Diary of a Tuscan Bookshop

A Memoir

Alba Donati

Translated by Elena Pala

Scribner

New York   London   Toronto   Sydney   New Delhi

Scribner
An Imprint of Simon & Schuster, Inc.
1230 Avenue of the Americas
New York, NY 10020

First Scribner trade paperback edition May 2023

SCRIBNER and design are registered trademarks of
The Gale Group, Inc., used under license by Simon & Schuster, Inc.,
the publisher of this work.

For information about special discounts for bulk purchases, please
contact Simon & Schuster Special Sales at 1-866-506-1949
or business@simonandschuster.com.

The Simon & Schuster Speakers Bureau can bring authors to
your live event. For more information or to book an event, contact
the Simon & Schuster Speakers Bureau at 1-866-248-3049 or visit our
website at www.simonspeakers.com.

Interior design by Hope Herr-Cardillo

Manufactured in the United States of America

1   3   5   7   9   10   8   6   4   2

Library of Congress Cataloging-in-Publication Data has been applied for.

ISBN 978-1-6680-1556-8
ISBN 978-1-6680-1558-2 (ebook)

To my wacky family,
made of dates and names that don't add up

Once upon a time there was a doll's house that belonged to a queen. A doll's house so marvellously made that from far and near people came to look at it.

Vita Sackville-West,
A Note of Explanation

Diary of a
Tuscan Bookshop

January

Every little girl is unhappy in her own way and I was too, deeply so. Maybe it was because my only brother got married and left us, all of a sudden, when I was just six years old; or because of my rather old-fashioned mother, or maybe that vein of rustic cruelty in my girlfriends at the time was to blame—one day you're in; the next you're out.

Since the day I opened the bookshop, Libreria Sopra la Penna, I've barely had a conversation where I wasn't asked, "How did you get the idea to open a bookshop in a village of one hundred and eighty souls, in the middle of nowhere?"

I've spent the day wrapping. A lady from Salerno chose to celebrate Valentine's Day like this: she got a book of poems by Emily Dickinson, an Emily Dickinson–themed calendar, and a fragrance with osmanthus base notes, also named Emily, for one of her daughters. For her other girl she got a different book by Emily Dickinson, the Emily Dickinson calendar again, and a bracelet made with rose and gypsophila petals. And on top of that she bought her beloved *Emily's Herbarium* and another calendar too, as a treat for herself.

How did I get the idea? Ideas don't just spring out of nothing—they smolder, ferment, crowd our mind while we sleep. Ideas walk on their own two legs, follow their own parallel path in a part of us we have absolutely no idea existed, until one day they come knocking: Here we are, they say, now listen carefully! The idea for the bookshop must have been lying in wait, ensconced in the folds of that dark and joyous country we call childhood.

I used to spend every afternoon at the home of my grandfather, who had one of those new radios with a cassette player—he wasn't that modern, mind you, Grandpa Tullio, but my aunts were. Modern and loose (or so said people in the village). I was a bit ashamed of that, but I adored them. At the opposite end of the spectrum sat Auntie Polda, my mother's sister, a bighearted farmer who, among other quirks, had never married and was proud of it. I spent days unbuttoning and re-buttoning her cardigans, just an excuse to sit on her lap really, and listen to her stories. And then there was my auntie Feny (Fenysia), who was a governess. Petite and strong, shy and wise, it was she who introduced me to reading, who brought me novels given to her by the rich families she worked for. The School of Languages and Culture, which I founded a few years ago with my partner, Pierpaolo, is named after her: nurturing knowledge felt as essential as making a good minestrone (just like Auntie Fenysia's).

My mother's stories, by contrast, were the stuff of nightmares. Her favorite was the tale of a little girl who fell asleep under a tree while her mother worked in the fields, and the big fat snake who saw her and slithered down her throat. Thankfully, I can't remember how the story ends, but it's safe to say my bruised subconscious would truly heal only much later, after twelve years of work with my therapist, Lucia.

Our village was small, and I adored it: I would draw the mountain opposite our house as if it were Kilimanjaro, in spring, summer, autumn, and winter. A philosopher might say that "elsewhere" is simply any place you've never been, and to this day I have yet to set foot on that mountain. I loved the fields covered in frost—they looked made of crystal to me, like something out of a fairy tale. And I loved ants, their endless struggle to stay alive. Because if you grow up in a house without central heating, without a bathroom, and your eyes, hands, and even your ears constantly play tricks on you, it's only normal to think you might die.

My father is missing from this neat family picture—and I did miss him a lot. When he'd sit next to my bed (which I often pictured being my deathbed), my eyes, hands, and ears would settle and the world was not such a horrible place anymore.

I happened to start this diary on January 20, the same date that features at the beginning of Georg Büchner's *Lenz*. Dates matter, and we all have our January 20, the day Lenz sets off and leaves everything behind. On January 20, 1943, my mother's first husband also set off—orders had just come in, for him and the other surviving men in the Alpini brigade, to abandon the front on the Don River and retreat. It was the tragic ending to Italy's military campaign against Russia, an ending that claimed 151,000 lives, either confirmed dead or missing in action. It was −40°C and many of those men didn't even have shoes. Iole, my mother, was twenty-four; her husband, Marino, twenty-eight; my brother, Giuliano, six months old. The family that could have been ceased to exist near Voronezh, where the Russian poet Osip Mandelstam moved with his wife before being sent to a concentration camp in Siberia, where he died. My mother waited, but no news came of Marino, as if he'd been swallowed by the steppe. Official entries on the war register end on January 23, 1943—after that, nothing. What did come was a war pension for the wives of all the missing soldiers.

Eventually, I would leave everything behind too: the most beautiful city in the world, a prestigious job, a comfortable flat near the National Library. I came back to my village, to see if the snake had left, and if that little girl asleep under the tree hadn't been Alice in Wonderland all along.

—

Today's orders: *The Adversary* by Emmanuel Carrère, *Lives of Girls and Women* by Alice Munro, *A Boy's Own Story* by Edmund White, *Leaving Home* by Anita Brookner, *Between the Acts* by Virginia Woolf, *Hotel Silence* by Auður Ava Ólafsdóttir.

January 21, 2021

The idea to open the bookshop knocked on my door one night, oven-ready. It was March 30, 2019. I had the space: there was a hill by the house where my mother used to grow lettuce and where I'd hang clothes to dry on a wire tied to two old poles. What I didn't have was the money: opening a bookshop is expensive. I had to come up with something.

When I was little, we had a huge attic. Our house was a reflection of our family—half home, half black hole. As you walked in you'd see the kitchen, then to the right a large room that my mother had partitioned using a green curtain with large pink ribbons (on the side that housed, depending on the day, either my bedroom or my deathbed), and to the left a small living room furnished in classic seventies style with table, chairs, and cupboards all made of chipboard, so shiny they looked even faker than they really were. Then there were two doors. One led to the basement, a place which alone was responsible for a good two extra years of therapy; the other door led to the attic.

There was something about the attic that made it unique. The first flight of stairs was made of perforated bricks (a job my father had started when we moved into the house), but then, as you turned a corner, the new steps ended and the original wooden staircase, which must have been a few centuries old, began. My father's love had run out. Every time I went up there, I prayed that the wooden steps would hold, that I wouldn't fall into the abyss where my old acquaintance the snake was surely waiting for me.

On that makeshift staircase, all that was left of my father's short-lived project, my dreams began. Because once I'd turned that corner, braved the five infernal rickety steps, and reached the attic, I was safe. I'd made it. I was in my kingdom. I would set up an imaginary classroom, each child with their notebook. I played the teacher and marked my own homework from a few years before. Or I'd read my own personal bible—the *Conoscere* children's encyclopedia published by Fabbri Editore, twelve volumes and four appendices. I think even my style preferences originated there— three pages were dedicated entirely to ancient Roman footwear, with which I was positively obsessed. I even bought two pairs of gladiator sandals—one golden, one snow-white—with laces that crisscrossed all the way up to the knee. I was about twelve, the same age as Lolita. Aside from that, the encyclopedia covered very serious topics:

- The Italian independence movement
- Saint Francis of Assisi
- From wood to paper
- Rome conquers Taranto
- Giuseppe Mazzini
- Reformation and Counter-Reformation
- The tonsils
- A genius named Leonardo Dante
- The Five Days of Milan
- Textile plants
- Japan

Knowing, for instance, that female Italian revolutionaries were re-
ferred to in their secret code as "our cousins the gardeners" made
me so unbelievably happy. It was like having a time machine, and
opening a page at random was like pressing the "go" button. I was
away, elsewhere: my favorite place. "We never test her; we're too
scared," my primary school teachers allegedly told my mother, who
for her part had abandoned the tale of the sleeping girl and the snake
in favor of a wide range of expletives. My father, meanwhile, had left.

I'm almost done wrapping the gifts for the lady from Salerno and
her two daughters. That's how I got the idea to open a bookshop in
a village in northern Tuscany, on top of a hill, overlooking the Apuan
Alps. I got the idea so a mother from Salerno could gift her daughters
two boxes full of Emily Dickinson.

—

Today's orders: *Ordesa* by Manuel Vilas, *El secreto de Jane Austen*
by Gabriela Margall, *Al giardino ancora non l'ho detto* by Pia Pera,
The Last Runaway by Tracy Chevalier, *Ghana Must Go* by Taiye
Selasi, *What You Can See from Here* by Mariana Leky, *La bellezza
sia con te* by Antonia Arslan, *Cuore cavo* by Viola Di Grado, *Hopper*
by Mark Strand.

January 22, 2021

One of the advantages of my new life is being able to hear the pattering of rain on the roof. In the city, if you're in bed, you have to
get up and open the curtains to see what the weather is like outside.
Here, you can sense it with your body. "For rain it hath a friendly
sound," as Edna St. Vincent Millay would have it, and here in our

village rain is like a voice—sweet at times, then louder—calling out to me. The phone rang today, and a different voice, prerecorded, completely inexpressive, informed us that a weather warning was in place for flooding and mudslides. This is bad news for the bookshop, because people don't feel like venturing up steep mountain roads in this kind of weather.

Lucignana sits on a hill five hundred meters above sea level, which is ideal if you want to be neither too hot nor too cold. The village was built entirely in stone before AD 1000. It used to have defensive walls and a castle, which must have been only slightly bigger than a large house. While the building itself is long gone, the name survives. Castello is what we call one of the tiny neighborhoods that make up Lucignana, alongside Penna, Scimone, Varicocchi, Piazza (the main square), Piazzolo (the smaller square), and Sarrocchino—many of these names are mangled versions of old toponyms: Scimone for Saint Simon; Sarrocchino for Saint Rocco.

Today, Castello is home to a friendly English retiree named Mike. He's ex-military; I have a feeling he was in Afghanistan. He built a swimming pool in his garden and in the summer he sits there in his birthday suit, much to the bafflement of his neighbors. When I go see him, he'll quickly wrap a towel around his waist and—in a profusion of "sorry, so sorry"—rush to put on some shorts. Then, with one of the most enchanting vistas in the whole world as his backdrop, he'll mix a couple of spritzers his way (which is to say, Aperol and lots and lots of Schweppes).

The view from his house really is something else: the Apuan Alps stretching before you, with sunsets so fiery you can picture the sun slowly dipping into the Mediterranean long after it disappears behind the mountains.

This is where, years ago, I wanted to set up a retreat for writers and translators. I fantasized about it for months with my friend

Isabella, another worker bee of the publishing world like me, but in the end nothing came of it. The house that belonged to Leo and Evelina Menchelli and their children, Antonio and Roberta, was snapped up by yet another English family. I'm very fond of the English, I should add—they'll buy and tastefully restore derelict buildings, improving where we Italians, in the past, have often made matters worse.

On the top floor of his house Mike keeps many lovely books in English; he gave me a few by Dorothy Parker and Sylvia Plath. He bought the "castle" from a fellow Englishman, although he bought it for his wife, who sadly passed away not long afterwards. It was she who said, "We didn't buy a house but a view." The books are hers.

One day, Mike came to the bookshop, sat at the back of the garden on one of the light blue deck chairs, and started reading *Everyman* by Philip Roth. He took it out of his backpack along with a flask and a large glass, into which he poured his homemade spritz with lots and lots of Schweppes. Like a Mary Poppins backpack, Mike's had everything he needed.

—

Today's orders: *Apprendista di felicità* by Pia Pera, *Miss Austen* by Gill Hornby, *Plainsong*, *Eventide*, and *Benediction* by Kent Haruf, *Diario delle solitudini* by Fausta Garavini, *The Alice B. Toklas Cookbook* by Alice B. Toklas, *La città dei vivi* by Nicola Lagioia.

January 23, 2021

The weather warning turned out to be correct. It rained all day, with a vengeance—or, in local parlance, it "wind-rained," which is to say buckets of water were hurled at the windows and most of the time the water seeped through. Initially I blamed Giovanni, the carpenter who refitted our windows and shutters, but it appears not much can be done about "wind-rain."

My thoughts are always with my little cottage full of books. I know they don't cope well with humidity and low temperatures—I can picture them shivering, their covers curling up in protest, fearing they've been abandoned. On sunny days, by contrast, when even the door is left wide open, I can see them smiling, grateful.

Looking after them is my new job. I worked in publishing for some twenty-five years and looked after many writers, but that was different—I didn't choose the writers; they were assigned to me. I read the books I had to read for work. I'd built a respectable career, culminating in the offer to lead the press office at a big publishing house. But the opportunity came too late—I had a young daughter and was anxious about relocating to Milan, so I turned it down. Madness. They ended up offering it to me as a remote position, which made me very happy. I wasn't going to do well in a nine-to-five office job. The anarchist in me craved something more unorthodox.

I was responsible for several authors. I couldn't believe my luck when they assigned me Michael Cunningham, Daša Drndić, and Edward Carey.

Michael is a very handsome man. Once, I was supposed to meet him in Mantua for a long TV interview, but he never showed up. He was staying in a palatial suite overlooking Piazza delle Erbe. I managed to slip inside this mansion with the cleaners' help. We found his room but couldn't hear a thing—complete silence. After much deliberation, the cleaners and I decided to ring the bell. Still nothing—not a sound. I'm usually a very positive person, but I was beginning to fear the worst. After further deliberation, we decided to get in. What I saw in that room I will never forget. The window, slightly ajar, let in a ray of light that gently caressed Michael's body—he was sleeping like a baby, naked, wrapped in a white sheet in this beyond-opulent bed. I thought of Giambattista Marino's verses, of Venus, who happened upon a sleeping Adonis and fell in love with him:

Rose: a lover's smile, made in heaven.

Another time, June 2014, I think, Cunningham was staying in Valdarno with Baroness Beatrice, widow of the Austrian writer Gregor von Rezzori. We were celebrating the latest edition of the Rezzori literary prize in a beautiful garden with white rosebushes so tall they were practically trees. My daughter, Laura, was there too, and her friend Matilde.

"Come, I'll show you the most beautiful writer in the world."

I always have copies of *The Hours*, *A Home at the End of the World*, *Specimen Days*, and *Flesh and Blood* in my bookshop. Now, in this rain, I hope Michael's books will be sleeping soundly like Adonis, waiting for the sun, for spring, for roses.

—

Today's orders: *The Diary of a Bookseller* by Shaun Bythell and *Al giardino ancora non l'ho detto* by Pia Pera, *Autumn* by Ali Smith, *Le Poids des secrets* by Aki Shimazaki, *La quercia di Bruegel* by Alessandro Zaccuri.

January 24, 2021

I took Dad to the optician's. He is almost ninety, lives alone, and his only pastime is reading *La Nazione*, a newspaper. The prospect of him losing his sight is so painful to me that as soon as we got the chance I dragged him in to be examined. The problem is the optic nerve in his left eye, which was damaged by Dad's latest stroke. It should be pink, but it's now white. I wish I could call an electrician, like Luigi who worked at the cottage, and ask him to replace the nerve, maybe rewire it with one of those cables of his—there has to be a way to fix an optic nerve, right? No, it turns out there isn't. But Dad didn't lose heart; he actually said the examination went well. We got him some new glasses and he's ready to read the day's news.

Dad is an important character in the story of my bookshop. It was he who taught me to read when I was five, and by the time I turned six I could already write letters to my auntie Feny, who was working as a governess in Genoa. Like everyone around these parts, Dad was born into a poor family, the eldest of six: Rolando, Valerio, Aldo, Maria Grazia, Valeria, and Rina—each more eccentric than the next.

Dad was born in 1931, but during the war he worked just as hard as the grown-up *partigiani*. He listened to the BBC's Italian-language radio broadcast and declared himself an anti-fascist. Everyone in the village was an anti-fascist. Lucignana is rather exceptional in this respect: we never had any deference to those in power. Legend has it that Lucignana was the only place in the whole of Italy where no one was affiliated with the Fascist Party. Officials would come from the council, all suited and booted in their uniforms, only to find the village deserted: people would run out to the fields or hole up in log cabins and smokehouses to avoid being forced to sign up for the dreaded party membership card.

Dad is very proud of our defiant spirit, and loves to tell the story of how, at 6:30 p.m. on September 8, 1943, General Eisenhower announced the Armistice with Italy on the Allied radio, followed by Field Marshal Pietro Badoglio's own announcement on Italian state radio at 7:42 p.m. The Armistice meant a break with Nazism, which was very good news for twelve-year-old Rolando. Lucignana's day had come at last: people gathered on the ridge above Canovaglio and lit a bonfire that could be seen by everyone down in the valley, where there was no shortage of Fascist Party cards.

But that's not where the war ended for young Rolando—the worst was yet to come, that moment when history intersected with an extremely painful wound in his family.

After the Armistice, the refugees who had fled to the mountains were making plans to go home. Lucignana had been hosting a family from Terzoni who were now getting ready to return to the valley, with their crockery and cows in tow. They asked Aurelio Moriconi, a fifty-something man, for help. Il Moriconi, as they called him, accepted, and for whatever reason he decided to take young Rolando and little Valerio along for the ride. The two brothers must have been very excited to feel useful, like the grown-ups. When they got to the river, however, they encountered an obstacle: there were no bridges on the Serchio. Luckily, they met some Brazilian soldiers from the Smoking Snakes brigade, who in those days were fighting to liberate Italy under U.S. command. As well as giving away cigarettes and chewing gum, the soldiers helped out with just about everything in the valley, so they got to work to build a crossing with some tree trunks. The cows went first—they slipped and had to be pushed back onto the trunks, jittery like hens with a fox in the coop. Not exactly the joyride Rolando and Valerio had pictured. Their turn came. Moriconi stepped onto the makeshift bridge holding their hands, then heard a thundering noise. It wasn't a plane, or a tank—it was water. Water that came at them at the speed of light, carrying them away. The Germans had blown up a dam upstream and the river had burst out into the valley. Young Rolando, who was just one step behind his brother, saw everything. The soldiers jumped in and reemerged holding something—it was Aurelio Moriconi. But little

Valerio's hand wasn't clasping Rolando's anymore. His body would be found three months later near Decimo, ten kilometers farther down the valley, wedged against an anti-tank barrier. Young Rolando didn't go home that night, and from then on every night brought fresh pain and sadness.

That's why Rolando can't afford to lose his sight—he has to read the news every day, looking for redemption. History repeats itself, and this time, if he sees it coming, he might just change the ending.

—

There were no orders today, so I took some time to finish *Why the Child Is Cooking in the Polenta* by Aglaja Veteranyi.

January 25, 2021

Today the children of Lucignana came to the bookshop after mass. It's always such a joy to see them approach as a group. They're the reason we do what we do, the invisible bridge that links our childhood to theirs.

As a little girl, I would brave the brick and wooden steps to get to the attic, where I ceased to be a little blob of mud and fears and became a person in my own right, building my identity one book at a time. If I hadn't had the attic I might have actually died, perhaps under a tree, with a snake down my throat. Up there I kept all my childhood memorabilia: coats, notebooks, fairy-tale books, schoolbooks, clothes gifted by relatives in the United States (I had no idea who they were), and even a talisman. The talisman was my father's suitcase, where, I presume, my mother had angrily shoved the clothes Dad had left behind. I opened it every day, studying the shoes, the cotton undershirts, the shirts. I didn't know if that suitcase would bring my father back, but I did know that it could keep pain at bay: he was there, protecting me.

Lucignana was looking for its own attic. The arrival of the bookshop on December 7, 2019, was a real event around here. The schoolteachers from Ghivizzano told me how proud the children were, even the "difficult" ones like Alessio and Matteo: "We have a bookshop," they'd said. This tiny village, little known even by people from nearby towns, was now in the papers and on TV, and everyone was talking about it. Visitors would hire coaches from far and wide, from Vicenza or Reggio Emilia, or they'd come in camper vans, large groups from all over Tuscany. Covid hadn't hit yet—or rather, it had, but we didn't know.

Today we saw the children come in through the garden gate, all wrapped up in hats and scarves. Sofia, a little blond girl with blue eyes, chose *Little Women* as a birthday present for a friend. Her brother Paolo, also blond and with blue eyes, a book about pirates. Little Anna picked up *La regina delle rane* (*The Queen of the Frogs*) by Davide Calì and Marco Somà, and Sara a copy of *Alice's Adventures in Wonderland* illustrated by John Tenniel. Watching them leave with the books tucked under their arms was really moving.

Emma and Emily were also part of the group. When I see them stroll around the village, side by side, I'm always struck by how they seem to walk at a different pace, out of sync with everyone else. Emily knows this, and every year she buys the Emily Dickinson calendar.

Then there's Angelica, who is twelve. Angelica is the reader. A willowy gymnast, she often does shifts at the bookshop and is always looking for a "different" book—when she says "different" she narrows her eyes, leaving this world behind and traveling back in time.

Angelica is me finally revisiting my childhood without fear. Because childhood is a trap: there are beautiful things and ugly things; you just have to find a magic wand to turn one into the other. Now that I've got my cottage full of books, I have nothing to worry about.

This reminds me of a beautiful message from Vivian Lamarque, one of my favorite poets, about the bookshop: "How wonderful!" she said. "What a marvelous idea! It's like Virginia Woolf's country retreat, only something a very young Woolf would imagine, say aged four or five."

—

Today's orders: *Lolly Willowes, or The Loving Huntsman* by Sylvia Townsend Warner, *Last Things* by Jenny Offill, *Teach Us to Sit Still* by Tim Parks, *Elizabeth and Her German Garden* by Elizabeth von Arnim, *The Green Wiccan Herbal* by Silja, *Wild Decembers* by Edna O'Brien.

January 26, 2021

That inexpressive voice on the phone again—apparently, temperatures will plunge overnight, and a weather warning is in place for ice on the roads. It feels like living on the set of *Twin Peaks* as David Lynch imagined it, at the border between the United States and Canada. Except here in Lucignana, Laura Palmer is alive and well and she opened a bookshop. A bookshop made of sticks, like the house of the second little pig in the famous fable.

Years ago I read a book called *Istruzioni per l'uso del lupo* (The Big Bad Wolf: A How-to Guide) by a young Emanuele Trevi. It's a tiny booklet, only a handful of pages, but it packs a lot of wisdom. I should use it as wallpaper for the bookshop. In short, Trevi writes, there's nothing to be done about the wolf: the wolf will come and blow our house down anyway. So you might as well do as the first little pig did, and face him down from behind a straw wall.

That said, I couldn't quite build a bookshop out of straw. So I called my friend Valeria, who is an architect in Florence (but her English boyfriend lives closer to us, in Lucca)—Valeria brought back to life all the houses I restored. I asked her to design a wooden cottage.

She came over to inspect the site, and when she saw where I'd planned to build my wolf-proof fortress she lit up. She likes challenges—she's one of those architects who will always find a way. I fell in love with her standing before a wall where different types of paint were being tested—we always liked the same hues. Dusty colors, noncolors, and lots of light. And so it was that she ended up working on three of the houses I lived in and we became friends.

The "site" measured twelve square meters on a craggy little hill, perched on a steep slope dotted with slanted olive trees. I'd send her photos of dainty bookshop corners from the UK, from France, from the Netherlands, photos of garden furniture from Provence, photos of gates, handles, chairs, lamps, light fittings, flower beds, and flower-draped ladders; photos of teacups and cute little coffers. I firmly believed it was all in the details. Poor Valeria had to deal with geologists, engineers, and iron rods while I sent her pictures of garden paths and elves' cottages at three o'clock in the morning.

We were so excited the day we could finally see the outline of the walls and ceiling, when the carpenters nailed the first wooden planks to the iron platform designed to expand the base of the fledgling bookshop. The second little pig wasn't so lazy after all; he had good taste: the wooden house was the most beautiful. Trevi didn't put that in his book; I must write to him.

He was right about everything else, though: the Big Bad Wolf will come one day, and he'd be paying us a visit soon enough.

—

Today's orders: *Vita meravigliosa* by Patrizia Cavalli, *In comode rate* by Beatrice Zerbini, *The Baltimore Boys* by Joël Dicker, *L'amore e altre forme d'odio* by Luca Ricci, *L'istante largo* by Sara Fruner, *A Winter Walk* by Henry David Thoreau.

January 27, 2021

A year ago we organized an event to mark Holocaust Memorial Day and a dozen children attended. Eleonora, a local Greta Thunberg who lives near Lucignana, read out a story in her sweet voice, and children were then asked to draw what they remembered of the story. Aside from Angelica, who as always was extremely focused and empathetic, I was struck by the reaction of a boy who suffers from ADHD. Matteo's eyes were wide open, and he was completely absorbed by the exercise. Yet another spell cast by literature.

As you open the sage-green gate and step into our garden, you find yourself inside a fairy tale (or so say our visitors). There's a wild plum tree, a peach tree, a leadwort bush, wisteria, roses, and peonies. Tables and chairs are made of wrought iron, and we also have two light blue Adirondack chairs and two flowery sun loungers.

The Adirondack chairs are very popular; some people will even reserve them. They were designed in the early twentieth century by Thomas Lee, an architect who spent his summers in the Adirondack Mountains, near the border between the state of New York and Canada. With time, they became "the" deck chairs.

Upside-down teacups hang from our trees, alongside lanterns that flicker on at sunset. There's also a little birdhouse that I painted myself, green and blue. But the birds never came. I'd taken it very personally until my brother, an experienced hunter, explained that the birds stayed away because of the cats. The cats belong to Luisa, who owns a shop right next door—there are quite a few. You never see them during the day, but at night the garden belongs to them. Luisa and her sister, Anna, were childhood friends of mine. Then there was Alda—but that's a sad story.

Holocaust Memorial Day to me is synonymous with Daša Drndić. Daša was one of the authors I was looking after when her book *Trieste* was published in Italy. Croatian, ballsy, and beautiful, Daša was a communist in the purest sense of the term. It was rare for her to like someone. She'd been in a relationship with the greatest writer, Danilo Kiš, and considered everyone else a spoiled brat. We became close and she wanted to translate my poems into Croatian, but then she passed away. She died on June 5, 2018. Two years before, she'd agreed to spend two weeks at the Santa Maddalena writers' retreat just outside Florence, run by the Baroness Beatrice von Rezzori. A wonderful place, were it not for the staff, who were all in uniform—Daša could not comprehend how a group of writers in their thirties could be waited on for breakfast, lunch, and dinner. I still have a photo of her doing the dishes after eating lunch with me at my house.

In *Trieste* you'll find forty-three pages containing the names of the nine thousand Italian Jews murdered between 1943 and 1945. Two pages with the Levi surname alone. Daša describes how Trieste's Risiera di San Sabba (previously a rice-husking facility) was used as a concentration camp, shining a light on the Nazi occupation of northern Italy after the Armistice. It's a book you must read. When it was published, I found myself talking about it with friends who argued that concentration camps had not been used to exterminate Jews. Friendships, too, can end.

—

There were no orders today.

January 28, 2021

Yesterday I phoned a real bookshop in Florence—the biggest, even. I wanted to know if they had any Emily Dickinson calendars in stock. I've run out and they're very popular, not just with our own little Emily. I still have one from 2001, the year my daughter, Laura, was born. I can't even find them on Amazon, so they really must be out of stock everywhere. My supplier marks them as "dispatched," but there's no sign of the actual calendars so far.

"Hello, I was wondering if you had any copies of the Emily Dickinson calendar."

Silence.

"I'm sorry, whose calendar?"

I'm always surprised when I come across someone who works in a bookshop and doesn't recognize a famous author's name. Emily Dickinson was not a name she'd heard before. It's like working in a bakery and not knowing what a Sacher torte is. Maybe she usually works in the science books section and answered someone else's phone. Yes, that must be it.

I always tell the volunteers who do shifts at the bookshop: "Have a look around: familiarize yourselves with the titles, the authors, the sections." One day in September a girl showed up.

She came alone, from the big gate at the back of the garden. Tall, very pretty, very long black hair. Without hesitating she walked up to me and said:

"I want to be a bookseller. I'd like to work here, even as a volunteer."

Her name is Giulia: she's half-Tuscan, half-Sicilian, knows a lot about books, and is currently studying engineering, although it's not what she wants to do with her life. She's not on Facebook or Instagram, which rather complicates our professional relationship but also instantly ranks her as a personal icon of mine. The way she showed up in the garden and just asked point-blank for what she wanted was yet another magic spell cast by our little bookshop. A parallel universe where strange things are set in motion: warnings, recommendations, shelves that reorganize themselves. Here Wendy goes to the ball instead of Cinderella, Cruella eats the poisoned apple, and Prince Charming saves the Little Match Girl from the cold. Anything can happen in our world. I told Giulia she could work at the bookshop. Giulia knows I'll need an Emily Dickinson calendar before I realize we've run out. Sometimes, wise beyond her years, she'll say something like, "Do you really need Terzani's essays? Come on, send them back."

And I send them back.

Brilliant young people fascinate me. But she's right, of course— we have "our" books, not the books you'll find everywhere. It's like your own bookshelves at home: whether recent or old, books need to make sense; they need to be chosen and live there for a reason. An arbitrary choice, perhaps, like separating male and female authors. It just came to me. Come to think of it, however, isn't it a relatively recent development for women to be professional authors? And if we're suddenly able to make a living from writing after centuries of silence, we probably have a lot to say, and will likely say it in our own, distinctive way. So isn't it logical that female authors should have a couple of bookcases of their own?

—

Today's orders: *The Penelopiad* by Margaret Atwood, *Cuore cavo* by Viola Di Grado, *Hopper* by Mark Strand, *The Family Carnovsky* by Israel Joshua Singer, *The Bookshop* by Penelope Fitzgerald, *I migliori anni della nostra vita* by Ernesto Ferrero.

January 29, 2021

Yesterday morning I felt things would actually turn out OK, despite the pandemic altering our daily routines. I got a pack of strange tarot cards called the Literary Witches Oracle, each card representing a famous female author. I ordered only one, to see what they were like, but I'll order more today. I'm sure our followers, who are mostly women (the women to men ratio is 85:15), will love them.

I picked up three cards at random: Anaïs Nin, "the subconscious"; Emily Brontë, "fantasy"; Jamaica Kincaid, "history." So here's my prophecy: we have to revisit our broken dreams, let our creativity run free, and realize our desires here and now, at this point in history.

There are thirty cards in total, created by Taisia Kitaiskaia and illustrated by Katy Horan. Some really captivate me. Sylvia Plath wears a black blouse, with fine red lines branching out from her waist—they could be roots, or veins, blood-pumping arteries. She represents "the dark." Flannery O'Connor ("humanity") hugs one of her peacocks. They'll sell well; I must get more.

But that's not the only good news from yesterday. I got an email from Natalie, a lady from Israel who makes stockings with quotes from *Pride and Prejudice* and *Alice's Adventures in Wonderland*, in the colors that Valeria and I like—dusty, lunar hues. I'd reached out to her a week ago; now we're negotiating an initial order of thirty pairs. I know a few customers who'd snap them up in a heartbeat—like a girl who came in one day, wearing a skirt that was an exact replica of the cover of Sébastien Perez and Benjamin Lacombe's *Facéties de chats* (The Secret Lives of Cats). She bought all her Christmas presents at the bookshop, twenty-seven in total—as well as Perez and Lacombe's book, of course.

This is what I fill my shop with—books and objects inspired by books. I wander the Web, browsing and browsing until the right thing materializes in front of me. What I call silent books, however, I found in person during a visit to MoMA in New York. They're exquisite rice-paper notebooks, hand bound; you can feel the twine along the spine. The covers are extremely refined replicas of cult book covers, such as *Breakfast at Tiffany's* or *Moby-Dick*, and the edge painting is completely artisanal too—Prussian blue or terra-cotta. I was already dreading arranging a shipment from New York to Lucignana when I found out they were handmade in Florence.

Yesterday I took a quick trip. With Donatella, I went to Coreglia (the seat of the council) to see Leonardo and Federico, who live in Villa La Penna. Walking in, you'd fancy yourself in Monk's House, Virginia Woolf's country retreat in East Sussex. Donatella is an ideal companion on these occasions; we like all the same things, and she takes lots of photos of various details. She's very good at that—you should see what she can accomplish with that phone of hers. To be perfectly honest, Donatella is very good at everything, and she has impeccable taste. She's beautiful, too, the most beautiful girl I know. Her house is beautiful. Her garden. Her husband, Graziano. Her daughter could be her sister. Two years ago, after the launch of my latest poetry collection, she came up to me and said something really special. I didn't expect it from her—she usually keeps her own counsel—and the way she talked to me was quite refreshing. Today we're like sisters. I picked up a tarot card thinking of her. It was Toni Morrison, "power." But if you ask me, the word for Donatella is "love."

—

Today's orders: *Ordesa* by Manuel Vilas, *Out* by Natsuo Kirino, *Hotel World* by Ali Smith, *Hotel Bella Vista* by Colette, *Kitty Foyle* by Christopher Morley, *My Turn to Make the Tea* by Monica Dickens, *The Penelopiad* by Margaret Atwood.

January 30, 2021

It is 4:59 a.m. This time last year the bookshop was burning and I didn't know yet. But I would before long. At 5:30 someone shouted outside my window: "The bookshop is on fire!" The Big Bad Wolf had caught up with us.

It was Alessandra, one of the volunteers who work at the bookshop, who came to alert me. Her husband, Claudio, was heading to the factory for his 6:00 a.m. shift when he saw the smoke. Her son Michele had just finished his shift and was on his way back home—a family relay.

"Go and check on the bookshop; I saw smoke coming out of there."

"The bookshop is on fire!" said Alessandra—those were her exact words.

I rushed downstairs, knowing full well I wouldn't be of any help. I just stood there, watching, as Michele opened the bookshop door and flames burst out and Alessandra carried buckets of water. It was all over in a matter of minutes.

Michele, tall and blond, had put out the fire and saved the day.

All I could do was message Pierpaolo, my partner, and Donatella, who arrived shortly afterwards with her husband, Graziano. We were all in our pajamas. Graziano, who heads the maintenance department of a large factory in the area, checked that there were no live wires in the tangle of cables around the beams.

The left side of the cottage was completely destroyed. The coffee machine had melted, the shelves had burned, and the charred remains of the books littered the floor. A sad dawn. By eight o'clock word had got around, and our friends gathered outside. Because that's how the bookshop came to be in the first place—it was a project shared with 70 percent of the village, volunteers doing shifts so that there would always be three people around at any given time: one manning the cash register, one to welcome visitors, plus myself doing a bit of everything. There wasn't much left for me or anyone to do now.

And thus ended the fairy tale of a poet who launched a crowd-funding campaign on Facebook to open a bookshop in a tiny village in the mountains.

Then something unexpected happened. By nine o'clock, the fire had already made the news and various journalists were heading to Lucignana. Some suspected it was arson. I went back home to make some coffee, followed by Barbara and Rosita, who had been with us since the beginning. We hugged, tears pricking our eyes. But that lasted only a few seconds.

"So what time shall we meet to tidy up?" I looked at my watch. "Ten?"

"OK. See you in a bit!"

And that's how we started over, together. The sun was shining on January 30, 2020. Barbara, Donatella, Rosita, Moira, Monica, and Fabiola wiped the blackened but intact shelves. The surviving books were being relocated to the garden—tall, dark piles snaking up the tables. Tiziana, or the mayor of Lucignana, as we call her, coordinated the volunteers. The younger girls turned up too: Noemi, Marika, and Elisa, Emily's mother, who was eight months pregnant. Armed with cloths and spray cleaner, we tossed what had to be tossed and wiped the covers of the books that could be salvaged, one by one. A plan was already taking shape: we would start another crowdfunding campaign and organize a sale for the battered but still readable books—no fixed prices, just people donating what they could.

Among the volunteers were two cousins, Giulia (an accountant) and Giacomo (an architect)—their enthusiasm is truly infectious. They are also the first people from Lucignana to have got a degree, and seeing them around the bookshop brought me so much joy. Giacomo (blue eyes, blond beard) is calm personified, while Giulia (bright black eyes) is always the one who will find a solution no matter what. To them I owe the energy and determination to start over. Because the bookshop didn't just rest on an iron platform—there was an entire community propping it up. And this, my dear wolf, is where your plan backfired.

—

Today's orders: *Apprendista di felicità* and *Il giardino che vorrei* by Pia Pera; *Le voci delle case abbandonate* by Mario Ferraguti, *La memoria rende liberi* by Enrico Mentana and Liliana Segre, *Insolitudini* by Marco Onofri.

January 31, 2021

This time last year we were in all the papers, double-page spreads and a picture of me looking rather disoriented, staring out from all the newstands in the district of Lucca. Barbara, Angelica's mother, was in all the photos too—Barbara who never wants to be in any photos. In her group of volunteers there are two Barbaras, both of them "imported," so to speak, meaning they came to Lucignana to follow a husband or a partner. That's why they were known as Daniele's Barbara and Maurizio's Barbara. The bookshop gave them back their surnames, and also helped create stronger ties between those who were born here and those who, like them, came later.

The bookshop—which opened on December 7, 2019, burned down on January 30, 2020, and reopened again in a flash—was also a catalyst for this group of people to become a real community. A community is like a special family where you help those who need helping and celebrate with those who have something to celebrate. Where you're always happy to lend a hand. Where you belong. And our family included carpenters, electricians, architects—it really was all hands on deck, and by March we were ready to reopen. For the occasion, the cottage had also acquired a pergola, which meant more space to display the books, and shelter from the sun and rain.

Meanwhile, the arson rumors slowly died out, banished by evidence of a short circuit which had melted the coffee machine along with everything else.

The day after the fire, around noon, I spotted a young woman of uncertain age wandering around the rubble in blue jeans and a coat that seemed too light for the season. Her name was Tessa, and she was looking for me. I would soon find out that she was Italian American, or rather: her mother, from the United States, was half-Irish, half–South African, and her father was Italian but originally from a German family. Her husband, named Christian, was from Nigeria. One woman, three continents.

Tessa drove from Lucca and parked her car by the bookshop. That morning, she'd gone to a local café for breakfast, where she read about the fire in a newspaper someone had left on the counter. She was on her way to deliver eight boxes full of books to some antiques shops in Lucca—the books belonged to her mother, who had passed away a few months before. When she read about the fire, however, she changed her mind and set off for Lucignana.

The books were in crates—the kind of crates they use to harvest olives, she was keen to point out, as if suggesting that books belonged with manual labor, with things like sowing and harvesting, and not with abstract ideas. I agree, by the way. Her mother is the key. She's the source of everything, the light that shines on everything, including the crates. We started unloading her car—Tessa with incredible strength and energy. I was a bit worried about all those beautiful books, which I had no idea where to store. She picked up on that.

"You look sad. What would it take to make you happy?"

I smiled. "Right now, ten thousand euros."

"Fine. I'll transfer the money to you this afternoon."

". . . ."

She hugged me, tears shining in her blue eyes.

"It's the money my mother left me—that's what she would have done with it. She taught us to help those in need. It was her mission in life."

Tessa gave us a bookmark, which is now our official bookmark. It reads: "It was my mother, Jean Martin, who taught me to look after other people. My father, Grenville, too, would always pick up strays along the road and give them a chance in life. He'd learned this from his own father, despite growing up in abject poverty."

It was signed by Tessa's mother, Lynn Holden Wiechmann.

Yes, her name was Holden.

—

Today's orders: *Hopper* by Mark Strand, *Mujeres que compran flores* by Vanessa Montfort, *Cuore cavo* by Viola Di Grado, *Il ragazzo selvatico* by Paolo Cognetti.

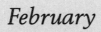

February

I went to Florence for a few days and didn't write anything. Impossible to write with my daughter, Laura, there, and with our dog Mirto, who replaced our beloved Kiko, who died last summer and is now buried under the plum tree by the bookshop, just outside the fence. With Kiko gone, there were no more enthusiastic welcomes, no more spinning around, no more whimpering to get me out of bed in the morning. I miss him.

Mirto is tall, springy, and muscly like a young wolf—he's Laura's dog, not mine. Her newfound maternal instinct is rather moving, as is the way she pursues her studies despite the rather rocky road she has traveled alone. I've always been around, but in the end, facing our fears is something we all have to do on our own.

My mother enjoyed living in Florence. After she turned ninety, she started spending several months with us there every year, from October to May. During those visits, she was transformed: no longer a farmer battling cold and hunger, she was an elegant lady who took long walks to Piazza Pitti and met friends for lunch. Once she was back from her social engagements, however, memories of Lucignana would fill our town house again in a flurry of phone calls with her childhood friends, who had long moved out of the village. Mery, sweet Mery, Romeo's daughter, now lived in Massa Carrara, and Redenta ("the marshal") in Genoa. They were forever bickering, and my mother would often find herself caught in the cross fire of their respective rants and accusations.

There's a beautiful novel by Rabih Alameddine, *An Unnecessary Woman*, in which the protagonist lives alone in a Beirut devastated by war, her sole occupation translating all the books she likes into Arabic for no apparent reason. The rooms are overrun with sheets of paper and books she has translated purely out of her love for literature. Every afternoon, in the apartment above hers, three friends meet to chat, put on makeup, and comment on life in the city—a chorus of sorts for the protagonist's solitude. I always imagined those three friends as my mother Iole, Mery, and Redenta, their voices a music that could be soothing or frenzied, and oh so necessary. Alameddine's is a novel I keep recommending even though it was published more than ten years ago.

—

Today's orders: *Too Much Happiness* by Alice Munro, *Il romanzo di Moscardino* by Enrico Pea, *Il rumore delle cose che iniziano* by Evita Greco, *Nehmt mich bitte mit: Eine Weltreise per Anhalter* by Katharina von Arx, *Jane Austen* by Virginia Woolf, *Le cose semplici* by Luca Doninelli.

February 5, 2021

In Lucignana, I am surrounded by a shadowy legion of long-gone aunts and uncles who scrutinize my every move. Auntie Polda watches the world go by outside her window, Auntie Feny warms up by the fire, her feet resting on the big flagstones. Then here's blue-eyed Uncle Fernando, who was still traipsing across the fields at ninety, and Uncle Ferruccio, whom I've never met since, I am told, he died young, carried away by a cable car to which he'd got accidentally attached. I never met Uncle Rodolfo either, he died young too. Uncle Aldo, our very own Peter Pan, left, breaking many a Wendy's heart under Australia's vast skies. Then there's Auntie Grazia, who in the sixties would lounge on a paddleboat in a bikini and straw hat at a time when women in Lucignana still wore headscarves. Last but not least, Cousin Morando, who was rather partial to wine, and who could be seen zigzagging up Lucignana's narrow streets on a Sunday morning, returning from his escapades in nearby towns.

On October 15, 1895, the Italian poet Giovanni Pascoli moved to a house not seven kilometers from Lucignana, along with his sister Maria. On June 5, 1897, he penned the introduction to his poetry collection *Primi poemetti*:

Was there ever a time when we weren't here? When I could not see, upon waking, the Pania massif and Monte Forato? And what is this voice? . . . It is the river they call Serchio. Tell me, Maria, my sweet sister, was there ever a time when we couldn't hear that voice?

Underneath all his flamboyant rhetoric, what Pascoli was saying was that he absolutely loved being here. He loved the landscape, and the people. He knew how much pain hid behind the beauty, behind the tranquility of everyday life. He knew about those who left, about their solitude in the endless New York nights, about migrants who whispered "cheap, cheap," pointing to the basket of chalk figurines they had to sell. Cheap, cheap, like fledglings who've fallen out of their nest, and cry out to each other, and recognize each other in the dark. Because this love Pascoli felt for our land was tinged with darkness. He writes:

Know that the drawn-out sweetness of your voices originates from the mysterious way they resonate within the deepest cave of your past sorrows.

I am yet to find a more accurate definition of sorrow.

Know that I couldn't see beauty the way I do now, were it not for the abyss I stared into before.

A century later, Seamus Heaney (who discovered Pascoli late in life, and admired and translated him) would go on to say similar things in his Nobel lecture, namely that in poetry, there must be room "for the marvellous as well as for the murderous."

I met Seamus Heaney. A genuine, very straightforward man, completely devoid of egotism, a poet. When I chose the name for my bookshop, Libreria Sopra la Penna, or Bookstore on the Hill, I thought of him. Lucignana never had any princes or barons—only serfs, sharecroppers, farmers, and farmhands. In Italian, *penna* translates as both "feather" and "pen," or "quill," but the *penna* our street is named after was most definitely a chicken feather.

In "Digging," one of his earlier poems, Heaney reminisces about his father digging potatoes out with his spade, and about his grandfather who, "nicking and slicing neatly," cut more turf in a day than any other man:

> But I've no spade to follow men like them. Between my
>   finger and my thumb
> The squat pen rests. I'll dig with it.

That's what I thought too.

I don't have the strength to keep chickens and grow vegetables, but I do have a pen—a chicken feather that turned into a quill and then into a pen. And I dig with it too, from my little bookshop between the Serchio and the Apuan Alps. Monte Prato Fiorito deserves a mention too because it is just so beautiful, although Pascoli couldn't see it from his house.

—

Today's orders: *La Canne de Virginia* by Laurent Sagalovitsch, *Le Temps du voyage: Petite causerie sur la nonchalance et les vertus de l'étape* by Patrick Manoukian, *Arabian Nights* illustrated by Marc Chagall, *The Missing Rose* by Serdar Özkan, *Diary of a Bookseller* by Shaun Bythell, *Apprendista di felicità* by Pia Pera, *The Vegetarian* by Han Kang, *Hokusai: Thirty-Six Views of Mount Fuji* by Amélie Balcou, *L'Oiseau blessé* by Ève Herrmann, *Alice Cascherina* by Gianni Rodari, *Forever* by Emma Dodd. Six Emily Dickinson calendars.

February 6, 2021

It's a sunny Saturday, so we're expecting quite a lot of visitors today—literature ramblers, pilgrims of the written word. Why come all the way up here? I often wonder. Because they're looking for something they can't find where they are. A girl who was hesitating between two books once told me, "I'll take this one; I haven't seen it anywhere else." I am truly privileged to be trusted with such important matters. But with great trust comes great responsibility—you can never let your readers down.

I can still remember every detail of that night in April, two years ago, when it all began. A word on the top right of the Facebook tab on my iPad caught my attention: "crowdfunding." I wasn't so much drawn to the "funding" element, but to the concept of crowd: a multitude of people. It instantly reminded me of "Crossing Brooklyn Ferry" by Walt Whitman:

Just as any of you is one of a living crowd, I was one of a crowd.

I sat up and started typing:

Title: "Opening a bookshop in a tiny village (Lucignana)." Description: "With just five euros from each Facebook friend I could make a dream come true: spark an inextinguishable passion for literature in a tiny village that doesn't even have a school (a bit like Juliette Binoche in *Chocolat*, but with books). The village is called Lucignana, only a few kilometers away from dreamy Garfagnana, and it's here that I want to open a little bookshop—say, a tiny wooden cottage open six months a year where children (but also adults) can find a book that speaks to them, a magical place where you can admire the most wonderful sunsets on the Apuan Alps."

I then typed in my bank details and other practical information. We asked for seven thousand euros. It was around six in the morning when the first donations started trickling through, and shortly afterwards we'd cleared our target. One hundred and seventy-five donations on Facebook alone; then there were those who'd come up to me in the street and stuff a twenty-euro note in my pocket. Others sent cash by post, or transferred money directly to my bank account. I'd raised about ten thousand euros thanks to an idea inspired by dear old Whitman, who was large and contained multitudes. What a wonderful word "crowd" is.

On April 13, I received a considerable donation from an Italian

American lady. This is what she wrote to me on Facebook: "My father was born in 1913 and remained in Lucignana until 1930. Your *nonna* might remember him . . . Enrico Panicali."

The bookshop was already everywhere, before it even existed. It had begun casting its spells when it was only a craggy little hill, home to a few heads of lettuce, two rusty poles, and a wire where clothes hung to dry.

—

Today's orders: *L'istante largo* by Sara Fruner, *Senti che vento* by Eleonora Sottili, *Sorelle* by Ada Negri, *Apprendista di felicità* by Pia Pera, *Ordesa* by Manuel Vilas.

February 7, 2021

Rain is predicted today, so we'll be closed. Yesterday the sun drew in crowds from Florence, Pistoia, and Pisa. A girl came to scout out the bookshop and will be back with a group of friends. Who is our typical visitor? you might wonder. Female, for starters. Voracious readers aged fourteen to seventy-five, although our strongest demographic is thirty to fifty. Then there are children—catering to them is easy: pop-up books about frogs, kittens, pirates, and ballerinas. Teenage boys, however, have mostly eluded us so far—we are yet to find something that will capture their imagination. We've tried all the usual suspects: *Gulliver's Travels*, *White Fang*, *David Copperfield*, *Treasure Island*, *Twenty Thousand Leagues Under the Sea*, with little success so far. Maybe we should give Stephen King a go—we could do much worse than *Misery*.

Yesterday's visitors were readers after my own heart. They bought *Walking* by Henry David Thoreau, *Between the Acts* by Virginia

Woolf, *Pride and Prejudice* by Jane Austen, *The Baltimore Boys* by Joël Dicker, and *A Note of Explanation* by Vita Sackville-West.

Once upon a time there was a doll's house that belonged to a queen. A doll's house so marvellously made that from far and near people came to look at it.

Thus begins *A Note of Explanation*, which Sackville-West wrote for an astonishing doll's house Queen Mary commissioned in 1924: a perfect replica of Windsor Castle, complete with functioning drainage pipes and water closets in microscopic bathrooms, miniature bottles containing actual whisky, and miniature copies of works by Arthur Conan Doyle, Thomas Hardy, and W. Somerset Maugham. *A Note of Explanation* was itself written on tiny sheets of paper measuring 1 centimeter by 1 centimeter and this compact, witty tale of a misbehaving sprite languished in the doll's house miniature library until 2016, when the Royal Collection Trust decided to publish it with the Queen's consent.

There are no queens here in Lucignana, but people still come from far and near. And in the autumn, when the peach tree sheds its leaves outside the cottage, I really felt like I was in a fairy tale, and I was happy. Autumn is also when my daughter, Laura, was born: my very own contribution to the fairy tale, something else I created from nothing—no mean feat.

No queens, then, but we do have fairies, and quite a few of them. For starters, to get here you have to cross what my friend Anna d'Elia maintains is the mythical enchanted forest of Brocéliande, where Merlin is buried (although Brocéliande itself is no match for Anna, used to translating Antoine Volodine's impenetrable word thickets).

Beyond the forest live the fairies, and the bookshop belongs to them. A whole flutter of fairies.

One of the nicest is my cousin Fabiola, who lives just outside the village. Tiny and plump, she appears shy, quiet, and introverted, but looks can be deceiving. Her grandmother Egre was a force of nature. She'd married a meek man, my uncle Rodolfo, who died young, perhaps having realized he'd better get out of her way. Maria Pia, their daughter and Fabiola's mother, was somewhere in between—strong-willed, but nowhere near as much as old Egre.

When she was in high school, Fabiola would come over to my house to get help with her math homework (my first boyfriend was an architect). While he explained whatever concept she was struggling with, she'd be standing by the door, in silence, looking at her shoes. Then she ended up marrying Antonio, a six-foot hippy with long hair and a passion for innovative horticultural techniques. Once, he planted some twenty mirrors in the field behind their house, arguing that the reflected light would improve the potato harvest. They really are the perfect couple: she's forever fussing about everything, and always looks very prim and proper; he's incredibly laid-back, with a tangle of curls that will defeat any hair tie. They called their daughter Andrea, which is a constant source of confusion in a country where that name is usually reserved for boys. And in case you thought you had Fabiola figured out, one evening, as we were discussing same-sex marriages, she came out strongly in support of same-sex couples being allowed to adopt (which in Italy is as progressive as it gets).

Fabiola is, without a shadow of a doubt, one of the hapless fairy godmothers in *Sleeping Beauty*. Terrified of the powerful Maleficent, they mostly seem to flail about not achieving much, but in the end they triumph—and indeed, without them there wouldn't be a story. The most beautiful thing I've seen Fabiola do is cry. She cries over friends who battle with loneliness, over childhood memories, over people suffering. She specializes in spells for the good of all mankind.

Today's orders: *Call Me by Your Name* by André Aciman, *Claude Monet's Gardens at Giverny* by Jean-Pierre Gilson and Dominique Lobstein, *The Genus Rosa* by Ellen Willmott, *Le Bonheur: Essai sur la joie* by Robert Misrahi, *In Cold Blood* by Truman Capote, *Diario dello smarrimento* by Andrea Di Consoli.

February 8, 2021

The second crowdfunding campaign, the one we launched after the fire, ended up being even more moving and inspiring than the first. We had to rebuild half the bookshop, rewire the whole electric system, buy new books, lamps, mugs, teacups. A friend of mine named Luca wrote to me saying I should try GoFundMe, which I later realized was one of the most powerful fundraising platforms out there.

We set the target at €8,000, although we needed three times that sum. It didn't take us long to get to €8,422, and then one day someone reached out, saying: "You're on the GoFundMe home page! That's huge! How did you do that?" I hadn't done anything, and I didn't even realize it was such a big deal to be on the home page. Everything I know about social media I've learned on the job, so to speak—I've always just gone with my gut. All I can say is thank you, a thousand thank-yous.

Not all the donations came from the Web, however. There was Tessa, of course, and spurred by Graziano, many local entrepreneurs also contributed generous sums. I personally reached out to many publishers, asking them to each donate ten books to help me start over—they all did, aside from two. Maybe they had bigger concerns than a faraway bookshop on a hill. I can't blame them—Covid had just hit.

On March 3, 2020, *Buone Notizie* (Good News), a weekly supplement to the Italian newspaper *Corriere della Sera*, dedicated three whole pages to us. On the front page, a photo of me wheeling a barrow full of books up Lucignana's narrow streets, aided by Kiko.

On March 9, Italy's prime minister announced the first of many lockdowns. Shops, factories, and schools were shut, and everyone was confined to their council area. Incidentally, we used the English term "lockdown" even though there was an Italian equivalent available—we needed something the whole world could understand. We needed a big, clunky mammoth of a word, something that would make it easier for us to accept that the daily procession of coffins from Bergamo Hospital was our life now.

Being stuck in Lucignana brought us back to our childhood, to a time when happiness was found in the little things. Meeting Donatella and Tiziana for tea became a habit, as did painting furniture in the garden—chairs, benches, tables—while Kiko was still with us (as in that front-page shot). Our blacksmith gifted us two wrought-iron gates, in that pale, sage-green shade that Valeria and I love so much. They were even more romantic than the ones I'd gather on Pinterest and forward to Valeria in the dead of night. Giovanni, meanwhile, had rebuilt the burned-down bookshelves and the external wall—we were ready to go, but lockdown meant we had to wait.

Pierpaolo and I were making ambitious plans—with Tessa's donation, we could dream big. We'd been looking into a house—three floors plus basement—that overlooked the bookshop and the garden. It had been empty for decades. My only memory of it was that of Romeo, a big hulk of a man who'd sit outside the front door with an apron around his waist and a washtub tucked between his legs, sculpting chalk figurines (not unlike those, I imagine, the poor immigrants had to peddle on the streets of New York City). Romeo, incidentally, was Mery's father, and his wife, Teresina, a seamstress, taught my mother all the tricks of the trade. He was a pagan god of sorts, guarding the village gates—the house sits at a crossroads between the street that from the church leads down the hill, and our street (Sopra la Penna), which leads up to Castello.

After much deliberation, we took the plunge and bought it. The idea is for it to house a bookshop and a café, plus a little flat for the two of us, and another one for visiting authors and translators as well as friends.

—

Today's orders: *Our Souls at Night* by Kent Haruf, *Little* by Edward Carey, *Longbourn* by Jo Baker, *Teach Us to Sit Still* by Tim Parks, *Cactus: Meditazioni, satire, scherzi* by Alfonso Berardinelli.

February 9, 2021

It's raining. Temperatures are predicted to go down and snow is forecast for later. It is 7:30 in the morning and I'm writing from the little bedroom on the top floor, which used to be an extremely cluttered attic ("let's keep it; you never know!").

This house was refurbished by stealth. My mother was in Florence and had no idea work had started—work that would totally revolutionize the house we'd inherited from Auntie Polda and Auntie Feny. She is 101 years and ten months old today, and insists on washing paper napkins and paper towels, which invariably disintegrate—but she is almost completely blind and doesn't notice. When my niece Vania helped me clear the attic, we found tiny little bags with hundreds of mismatched buttons, ribbons, zippers, and lids. We were doing away with a whole world, and I felt a bit emotional. But in the end, where once was a century's worth of sorrow and buttons now sits a laptop (mine) and a nice balcony overlooking Monte Prato Fiorito.

The night is my kingdom. I often think of Alberto Manguel in his fifteenth-century barn-library in the south of France, of the nights he spends wandering among his forty thousand books, of the barn that leaves its material dimension behind and becomes pure light, illuminating many a reader's sleepless nights. This image comes straight out of Manguel's book *The Library at Night*.

Alberto is a beacon—thanks to him I discovered Edwidge Danticat, Annie Proulx, Helen Garner, Rose Tremain. He was Jorge Luis Borges's personal reader, meaning that at age nineteen, he found himself reading books out loud to a living legend who had gone blind. Alberto tells this story in *With Borges*, a little memoir I must order for my bookshop. I must also write to him and ask what he's reading right now—our visitors would certainly benefit from knowing that.

Alessandra will be here shortly—she's been helping me look after Mama every morning. Without her I'd be lost. I never felt loved by my mother, nor she by me—the conflict simply runs too deep; we cannot understand these feelings any more than we can eradicate them. Alessandra's was a difficult childhood—she, too, was unhappy in her own way. She ended up marrying Claudio, though, Lucignana's handsomest, and beating all the odds. They're a great couple: she has a potty mouth and sends lowbrow memes to the Lucignana girls' WhatsApp group, while tall, blond Claudio is politeness personified and you won't catch him swearing, not even by mistake. They saved the bookshop that morning, a year ago. Last summer, on holiday on the island of Giglio, Alessandra read a book, perhaps the first book she'd ever read. Claudio couldn't believe his eyes: to prove it wasn't all a dream, he took a photo and sent it to us.

Today's orders: *All Things Cease to Appear* by Elizabeth Brundage, *My Own Story* by Emmeline Pankhurst, *Miss Austen* by Gill Hornby, *Lolly Willowes or The Loving Huntsman* by Sylvia Townsend Warner, *Last Things* by Jenny Offill, *The Penelopiad* by Margaret Atwood, *The Missing Rose* by Serdar Özkan.

February 10, 2021

It's been raining all day; the garden will be a bog. It makes me sad. I have to call the gardener and ask him when we can expect the first new shoots of grass, the first new peonies and roses, when we should prune the plum tree and the peach tree (although Fabio, my great-nephew, will take care of the pruning himself). It's predicted to be sunny on Saturday and Sunday—fingers crossed.

There is a section in our bookshop I'm particularly fond of—biographies. Let's just say that, in the famous controversy between Sainte-Beuve and Proust, I've always sided with Sainte-Beuve: authors don't write in a vacuum; they draw from their own obsessions, from the lump of their emotions, from the void within them.

Why did the literary critic Cesare Garboli, for instance, fixate on Giovanni Pascoli, a poet he didn't admire? Because he knew there was something hiding below the surface, a secret that fed Pascoli's poetry, and he had to find out what it was. The secret had a name: his sister Ida, the "swallow," whose marriage threw Pascoli's life into disarray. He refused to go to the wedding, and locked himself up in his house writing seething, hurtful letters to Ida, who had destroyed the family home, the "nest" he'd so carefully rebuilt in Castelvecchio. How can that event not have influenced Pascoli's *Canti di Castelvecchio?* From this tangle of stories emerged *Trenta poesie famigliari di Giovanni Pascoli*, a masterpiece of literary criticism by Cesare Garboli.

Garboli, like Pascoli himself, would eventually leave Rome and move back to his family home in Vado di Camaiore, near Lucca. He died on Easter Sunday, April 11, 2004. Pascoli died the day before Easter, on Saturday, April 6, 1912. We were all in love with Cesare, really. Marinella, who worked at the Castelvecchio Archives, Andrea, who at the time was the head of the district council and kept showering him with appointments (risking the wrath of the good people of Lucca), and my good friend Sabrina, beloved colleague and partner in crime in my "golden years."

"I have to call Garboli and ask him to do something he won't want to do," Sabrina confessed to me once. "I think I'll call but won't tell him it's me."

So she put on a fake voice and picked up the phone:

"Good morning, Professor. I'm calling from Politeama Theater. We'd like to invite you to give a lecture on Molièr. . . ."

"Sabrina, please. You know I'm busy. . . ."

Once, in the summer, I went to see him in his house in Viareggio and he sent me to buy six bottles of mineral water. Behind his building you could see the warehouses where the sculptures for the famous Viareggio carnival parade are built every year. A gigantic Berlusconi caricature oscillated in the June breeze. I felt it was a bad omen, a message.

Among our biographies you'll always find various books about Emily Dickinson, Jane Austen, Sabina Spielrein, Vivian Maier, Daphne du Maurier, the Brontë sisters, Virginia Woolf, Vita Sackville-West, Colette, Zelda and Scott Fitzgerald, Wisława Szymborska, Frida Kahlo, and the Mitford sisters.

Last night I started *La Canne de Virginia*, by Laurent Sagalovitsch. Bizarrely, I was never curious about the last days of Virginia Woolf's life. I didn't want to know the details of how it ended. Around lunchtime on March 28, 1941, by the Ouse River, Leonard Woolf saw a walking stick. Hers. Virginia had drowned herself. She was lying on the riverbed, her pockets full of rocks. First, however, she'd planted her cane on the shore, firmly erect. As if to say, *I cannot carry on, but you must.* We do our best, Virginia. We do our best.

—

Today's orders: *Plainsong, Eventide*, and *Benediction* by Kent Haruf, *Desperately Seeking Frida* by Ian Castello-Cortes, *Due vite* by Emanuele Trevi, *Nehmt mich bitte mit: Eine Weltreise per Anhalter* by Katharina von Arx.

February 11, 2021

Today is a cursed day. Just before dawn on February 11, 1963, in her house at 23 Fitzroy Road, London, Sylvia Plath opened the window in her children's bedroom, then sealed the kitchen windows and stuck her head in the oven. On February 11, 1996, on Via del Corallo, Rome, the poet and translator Amelia Rosselli jumped off her balcony on the fifth floor of the building she had lived in for twenty years. Both had attempted it before; both had fantasized and written about it several times. Amelia had translated Sylvia's poems. Sylvia was thirty, Amelia sixty-five, Virginia fifty-nine. Strange how we end up fixating on these numbers and coincidences, as if they were messages in a bottle, cryptic cues we must decode.

I'd bought a copy of *The Bell Jar* from a book stand in Central Park—Plath's only novel, originally published under the pseudonym of Victoria Lucas. I got it for the bookshop, as well as two others from that same stand: *The Bell Jar* sat snugly between *The Year of Magical Thinking* by Joan Didion and *The Door* by Magda Szabó in a translation by Ali Smith. Together, they formed a totemic trio that I felt would protect us. Coming across three of my cult classics in the same place made me reflect on how love traces an inescapable path throughout our lives. Sadly, these books went up in flames with all the rest last year, but like Virginia Woolf's walking stick, we stood firm in the wind and rain.

The sun came out today, interrupting my somber reflections, and with the sun came Donatella. She came running, because she wanted to catch me before breakfast. Her smile and carefree energy are a good antidote for such mournful anniversaries.

Pierpaolo and Giulia will be coming too, from Florence. They've organized a "social media event," which is to say I'll be reading a few poems by Roberto Carifi, from his *Amorosa sempre* collection. Roberto suffered a violent stroke more than fifteen years ago, and now lives in Pistoia in a house that resembles a Buddhist temple. The various Italian poetry cliques only have eyes for Valerio Magrelli's mathematical precision or the esoteric verses of Milo de Angelis. As a bookseller, part of my job consists in remedying these editorial injustices by showcasing "alternative" authors, engaging in little but meaningful acts of defiance. Because as Carifi wrote in his *Amorosa sempre*:

Things won't forget
too solid their memory

After his wife's death, if Leonard Woolf happened to find a Bible in a friend's house he'd secretly slide it into his bag and once at home he'd burn it. He had prayed so much that he'd lost his faith. How wonderful it would be to steal the books that can muddle people's values and throw them into the fireplace! We shouldn't burn books, I know. I'd still like to claim it as a symbolic act of reparation though, an irreverent prank à la Pippi Longstocking.

—

Today's orders: *Il postale* by Vincenzo Pardini, *The Rose Garden* and *The Springs of Affection* by Maeve Brennan, *The Years* and *Jane Austen* by Virginia Woolf, *The Dark Traveler* by Josephine Johnson, *Nessuno può fermarmi* by Caterina Soffici.

February 12, 2021

The event didn't go as well as we'd hoped. We'd wanted to do the reading outside, in the garden, but the audio ended up being very poor. As well as the ceaseless vibrations of the wind, you could hear a symphony of tractors and chain saws in the background. That's the countryside for you—in the city we'd have had ambulances and streetcars. The next reading, we decided, would be indoors. Then, by way of consolation, we went upstairs for a cup of tea.

Tea is a crucial component of our bookshop experience, piping hot in winter and iced in summer. For our winter brews we use a variety of tea blended in Spain, with countless flavors. You can choose from different bases (black, green, red, white) as well as top notes of vanilla, bergamot, ginseng, mango, lime, turmeric, ginger, cinnamon, mandarin, honey, and lemon. The packaging is very eye-catching, with a bold, Mexican-style color palette. We nicknamed it Frida Kahlo tea.

Our teas from Kent couldn't look more different—they come in elegant collectible tins, emblazoned with the profiles of famous authors or literary characters. Jane Austen's is a blend of Chinese black tea and rose petals, Charlotte Brontë's a classic jasmine green tea. Alice in Wonderland's is a fruity extravaganza with chunks of strawberry, apple, hibiscus, elderberries, rose hips, and pineapple. Mary Shelley's is a favorite of mine (Sri Lankan black tea and violets), but I'm also partial to Little Women (a nod to red velvet cake—black tea with chocolate and vanilla).

Where quality tea goes, delicious jams are never far behind, and that's where we really knocked it out of the park. It all started with Anna, a charming lady who could be straight out of a Bernardo Bertolucci film. A cello player with the Maggio Musicale Fiorentino orchestra since 1983, Anna loves cooking. She goes by two different surnames—one as a musician, one for her culinary endeavors. Her gray eyes have a rare, timeless beauty. I don't know what sorcery hides in her hands, what guides them. It must be for those like her that Colette allegedly said:

> Cooking—real cooking—belongs to those who taste, who savor, daydream a little, then add a dash of oil, a sprinkle of salt, a sprig of thyme. To those who weigh without scales, time without clocks, watch the roast without looking. Those who mix eggs, butter, and flour following their inspiration, like a benevolent witch.

Anna and I came up with the idea of "literary jams." I studied and researched various authors' and characters' tastes, and Anna did the rest. For Virginia Woolf she created a bitter orange and whisky marmalade; for Jane Austen an apple, lime, and cinnamon compote; plum and star anise for Colette. For the Italian poet Dino Campana and his lover, the feminist writer Sibilla Aleramo, we sought out a variety of pear from a century-old tree that grows in a villa in Bivigliano, not far from Campana's hometown of Marradi in the Tuscan-Emilian Apennines. The little round "fox pears" were then left to stew in mulled wine. Our visitors love Anna's creations, and although she's been wooed by many, we agreed she would make them only for us.

—

Today's orders: *Autumn* by Ali Smith, *Elizabeth and Her German Garden* by Elizabeth von Arnim, *The Alice B. Toklas Cookbook* by Alice B. Toklas, *The Green Wiccan Herbal* by Silja, *Il gioco* by Carlo D'Amicis.

February 13, 2021

Yesterday, shortly after I wrote about Anna, she phoned me. We don't speak often, so it felt like one of those extremely charged coincidences. She told me about these great bitter oranges and tiny little apples she'd found—which means more Virginia and Jane compotes on their way.

After lunch my great-niece Noemi came, and announced she was pregnant (I'd known for a few hours already because Alessandra had told me). Noemi is twenty-three; she and Valerio have been together for six years. It's hard to keep track of our family tree; even people from Lucignana don't have it all figured out. There are nineteen years between me and my brother. He got married when I was six, and had Vania and Debora, who technically are my nieces but really are more like sisters given the age difference. Vania had three children: Fabio, David, and Noemi. Debora also had a daughter, Rebecca. Oh, and Fabio also has a son, Diego, who is now one. With my mother, that makes five generations of Donatis in Lucignana.

It's comforting to see some new arrivals in the village. Last year, as well as Diego, we had Samuele (who was still in Elisa's big belly when, on January 30, she was wiping blackened book covers).

The council is planning to build a little playground in Lucignana, except the only available space would be right next to the (ugly) war memorial. The village is split, as is often the case, roughly 70 percent in favor and 30 percent against. I even phoned my friend Bernardo, the abbot of San Miniato in Monte, who doesn't see where the problem is—according to him, having children play right next to an (ugly) war memorial is a symbol of peace and renewal. But that's Lucignana for you; there's always 30 percent who won't agree with anything. It was the same with the bookshop—some never liked the idea. It is what it is. There were even those who, shortly after we opened for the first time, took it upon themselves to hurl our flowerpots down the hill we call Il Poggione ("the big hill").

It snowed last night, two wonderful inches of white blanketing everything. The streets, however, are clear, and the weather's predicted to be good all day. According to Italy's Covid tier system we're in a "yellow" zone, where people can travel outside their council area—we're hoping for a busy day at the bookshop. Tomorrow, however, we're moving to "amber," which means we'll be confined to our own village, so we can relax with a good book.

I ordered all of Fannie Flagg's novels (the author *of Fried Green Tomatoes at the Whistle Stop Cafe*)—I love the romantic covers. I think Flagg is like a lighter version of Kent Haruf. He invented Holt in Colorado and she Elmwood Springs in Missouri—fictional towns that now exist in their own right, beyond the realm of geography. Both authors focus on completely ordinary lives, rather subdued in Holt, louder in Elmwood Springs. Little towns with their little problems, with that stubborn 30 percent you always have to reckon with.

A few hours ago, in the dead of night, I was dealing with an issue. It seems our delicious tea blends from Kent won't be coming after all. Julie wrote me an emotional email in which she explained that Italian customs officers were refusing to let their products through and all their parcels were being destroyed at the Poste Italiane "International Exchange Center." This really is a blow—no more Jane Austen and Mary Shelley tea; it's all being destroyed by customs, courtesy of Brexit. Italy won't be importing tea from the UK anymore. But I have my neighbor Mike.

He's in Brighton right now. I messaged him on WhatsApp at 3:01 a.m. and he answered straightaway. He told me he's been vaccinated and that the whole of the UK is under the strictest of lockdowns. I explained my predicament, and he offered to drive to Italy as soon as possible with our precious teas. He has a friend who lives in Kent, whom he plans to meet for dinner as soon as restrictions are lifted—he can swing by Julie's and pick up our tea. I love Mike; I love the way he thinks; I love the spritz flask and the glass he carries around in his backpack.

—

Today's orders: *The Other Woman* by Colette, *Ghana Must Go* by Taiye Selasi, *Al giardino ancora non l'ho detto* by Pia Pera, *What You Can See from Here* by Mariana Leky.

February 14, 2021

Yesterday I couldn't resist and went outside to take a few snaps of the bookshop, fairy lights twinkling in the hushed dimness of dawn. It was magical: snow decked our tables and marbled our cyclamens, and I swear that when I switched the lights on in the bookshop I heard a flutter of fairies scrambling out. Wandering around the tables in my fluffy slippers, I tried to capture that magic in my pictures.

Donatella and I opened early, but the first visitors arrived after lunch, when the snow had already melted. Shame. More good news came today—my great-nephew Fabio came to say hello with his cheeky little boy, Diego, and announced that he and Federica are having another baby. What's more, Federica and Noemi are perfectly in sync, both three months pregnant and due at the end of August. Our pool of potential readers is growing by the day. How funny, I thought—these children won't know Lucignana without a bookshop, will never comprehend the oodles of sheer insanity required to open one in a tiny village of one hundred and eighty souls, in the middle of nowhere. And I will be their bookshop auntie. We've been moved to the "amber" tier, so this will be a quiet Valentine's Day. The wind howled all night; there'll be plenty of broken tiles and fallen trees. Temperatures plunged, and the Surricchiana stream down in the valley roared in perfect tune with the wind—the poor little fawns in the forest must have been terrified.

Meanwhile, negotiations continue with Natalie, the Israeli seamstress who makes stockings with Jane Austen and Emily Dickinson quotes. I chase her; she seems interested, then disappears. But I'm not giving up— I must have those stockings.

—

Today's orders: *Welcome to the World, Baby Girl* and *Standing in the Rainbow* by Fannie Flagg, *L'istante largo* by Sara Fruner, *Nehmt mich bitte mit: Eine Weltreise per Anhalter* by Katharina von Arx, *Due vite* by Emanuele Trevi.

February 15, 2021

Yesterday two girls from Tereglio, a nearby village, came to the bookshop. One came on foot—a four-kilometer trek up and down various hills. The other wanted me to recommend novels by female

Italian authors, in particular Valeria Parrella, Teresa Ciabatti, and Nadia Terranova.

Of all the nearby villages, Tereglio is the one I feel is closest to Lucignana. In my mother's stories, they were forever going dancing in Tereglio when she was young, and Tereglio was also where Auntie Polda used to sell her butter.

A few years ago, a couple from Lucca, Massimo and Giovanna, fell in love with Tereglio. He quit his law firm and moved to the village, where they bought and restored various buildings and opened an inn. Thanks to them, Tereglio is now full of people after my own heart, people who appreciate a quiet spot to read in. One evening, in Lucignana's main square, Giovanna told me she had left the city thirty years before and had never looked back, not even for a second. Not even after Massimo had died. Giovanna has blue eyes, and more than enough charisma to go around.

I like Tereglio. Two rows of houses perched on a ridge, with a single street zigzagging up and down like a roller coaster. We should join forces—both villages would benefit from an alliance. For starters, we ought to restore the path Auntie Polda used to walk with her butter, which from the grove just behind Barbara's house (Maurizio's Barbara) led down to the river, then across the wooden bridge (which we'd have to rebuild), and finally up into Tereglio, right behind the inn, La Fagiana. Giovanna believes we should take the matter into our own hands, get enough people together and cut down the overgrown areas ourselves. We could put in an application for funds to the regional administration, but these things never actually materialize.

Today we had a family from Filicaia, another village in Garfagnana. They're all readers—mother, father, eleven-year-old daughter, and nine-year-old son. They debated for more than an hour which book to get the mother as her Valentine's present, while said mother sat in the garden enjoying the sun and the fresh air. In the end, they picked *All Things Cease to Appear* by Elizabeth Brundage, and she also got *Gli anni al contrario* by Nadia Terranova as a treat for herself.

We ended the afternoon with rose-hip tea, heart-shaped biscuits baked by Donatella, and honey fritters made by Tiziana. The pandemic (despite itself, I'm sure) gifted us these new rituals. It gave us our Sundays back; it gave us time with nothing to do and nowhere to be. Time for ourselves, for the little things.

Yesterday was a good day for Mama too. Irma, our neighbor, had done her hair up with curlers, and she looked really smart in the sunglasses I gave her last year. She spends all her afternoons with Ernesto, our other neighbor. Ernesto, originally from Florence, ended up in Lucignana for a series of complicated reasons linked to equally complicated relationships with the fair sex. He is seventy-five, lives off a meager pension in a house without central heating, and has a heart of gold. He adores my mother, and spends all (and I mean all) his afternoons sitting next to her on the sofa. Hand in hand, she confesses her deepest fears and shares her memories, while he goes on and on about the government or his favorite TV show.

In the afternoon, Mama often suffers from panic attacks, which she variously qualifies as "fear of leaving you" (me), "stomachache," or "a pain inside." Ten drops of Xanax and it's all over. Yesterday, her head softly resting on Ernesto's shoulder, I heard her mutter something about *The Count of Monte Cristo*, a book she read several years ago. My mother, who left school when she was nine, reads Dumas—books were in my DNA.

She had her fair share of darkness to contend with. When she was twenty, she married Marino, who was Egre's (my cousin Fabiola's grandmother's) brother. She got pregnant straightaway; it was 1942. Marino got leave from the army to visit little Giuliano after the birth, but he was nervous and dejected. He'd have preferred a girl—girls don't get sent to the front. Shortly afterwards he left for Russia, and no one ever told my mother he had died. But who, in fairness, could keep track of the thousands of corpses strewn across miles and miles of snow? "Missing in action" was the official line.

But "missing" is not as definitive as "dead." A few, who had managed to crawl their way back from Russia, said they saw him alive: not dead, they said, but not living either. My brother grew up with a mother and an army of aunts, but without a father. He's a grown man now, a grandfather, but when they erected the (ghastly) war memorial he fainted. I'm told that once, when he was about three, he'd climbed on a chair, leaned against the window, and, pointing at an unspecified spot outside, said: "Mamma, mamma, look, it's Pappà!"

—

Today's orders: *Asylum* by Patrick McGrath, *L'Enfance des dictateurs* by Véronique Chalmet, *An Unnecessary Woman* by Rabih Alameddine, *Stay with Me* by Ayòbámi Adébáyò, *La regina delle rane* by Davide Calì and Marco Somà.

February 16, 2021

I often wonder about this chunk of northwestern Tuscany where people say "*pappà*'" rather than "*papà*," where it "wind-rains" and lazy people are "lollers" or "slackies." Who were our ancestors, those men who lit a bonfire on a ridge on September 8, 1943, to spite the Blackshirts down in the valley? Lucignana's old guard was proudly anti-Fascist: Ghilardi, Pisani, Picchi, Ciribeo. And Auntie Polda too. Dad tells me that when party officials would come from Coreglia and parade through this godforsaken village without a single Fascist soul Auntie Polda would tag along and ape the Fascist salute, sashaying down the main street: "Attention!" Then there was Bruno Stefani, a thirty-year-old *partigiano* murdered by the Nazis near the church, right before his mother—what was he made of, what were they all made of?

I know—the way you know your deepest truths—that we share no bloodline with Florence. When the sun dips behind the Apuan Alps I know I am of those mountains. Forget ancient Rome and Etrurian pottery and the gently sloping hills of the Valdarno—this was the kingdom of the Apuan tribe, who settled on the mountains between Liguria and the slice of Tuscany subsequently named Lunigiana and Garfagnana. They were fierce people, sturdy workers, diffident and hot-tempered. The long-lost town of Apua, the heart of the kingdom, was probably located near modern-day Pontremoli. So what pushed them farther into the wilderness of the Apennines, on those rocky paths where you'd only come across wolves or bandits or both, as Ludovico Ariosto himself wrote after being appointed governor of Castelnuovo in Garfagnana in 1522? The Apuans were fleeing to remain independent; they were fleeing the Romans, who, having failed to tame them, decided to uproot them: in 180 BC, 47,000 Apuans were deported to a hilly area north of Naples.

But they didn't catch them all. A few must have managed to escape through some mountain gorge or other and reach Rocca Pectorita, a craggy outcrop jutting out above a sunny valley. There, perhaps, they began building a house—a large house, a house that could contain multitudes. Around AD 1000, the Lombards took over the area, and a church was built on that same site. Hermits resided there, and various beggars and pilgrims would shelter under its porticoes on their way to worship the Holy Face of Lucca, a wooden crucifix now found in Lucca's cathedral. The hermitage of Sant'Ansano sits on the hill opposite Lucignana, and like everything around these parts, you won't find it on popular tourist routes. The local authorities largely ignored it. All the valuables were pillaged years ago, but Sant'Ansano's beauty remains intact.

There's a path that leads from Lucignana to the hermitage through a holm oak forest. Inside, nothing has changed. Everything is exactly as the last hermit left it: the pallet, the washbasin, the chestnut table. My friend Bernardo and I have been planning a pilgrimage of sorts from the bookshop to Sant'Ansano—as soon as Covid allows, we'll organize it. Bernardo, incidentally, is the abbot Pope Francis requested for his personal "spiritual exercises" ahead of Easter two years ago. Bernardo's homilies are often inspired by poetry, and the one for the Pope was no exception.

There are a few authors who can paint a faithful picture of our people: Vincenzo Pardini from Fabbriche di Vallico, Maurizio Maggiani from Seravezza, and Fabio Genovesi from Forte dei Marmi. In his novel *Il mare dove non si tocca* (Deep Sea), Fabio describes an army of improbable aunts and uncles—unruly, rebellious, anarchic to the core. That's us to a T. Fabio himself, tall and lanky, wouldn't look out of place among Sant'Ansano's ancient hermits. If he ever comes to visit—and he will—he'll fall in love with this place.

Apuan women were apparently warriors too—as fierce, strong, and ferocious as the men. Centuries of Christianity have undoubtedly softened some of the sharpest edges, but the core remains intact. Alessandra drives into battle in her Citroën, Tiziana has an innate ability to fight stress, Donatella will disarm you with her smiles, our Barbaras (one extroverted, one introverted) are two Amazons, and so is Vania. Quite the army, in short, and our general is 101 years and ten months old. My mother.

—

Today's orders: *Hopper* by Mark Strand, *Olive Kitteridge* by Elizabeth Strout, *Tōkyō tutto l'anno* by Laura Imai Messina, *Il libro* *della gioia perpetua* by Emanuele Trevi, *The Bookshop* by Penelope Fitzgerald.

February 17, 2021

The arctic grip of winter has finally relented; today you don't even need a coat. I have eleven boxes full of books to return to my supplier in Genoa—I owe him too much money and I also need to clear out some space in the warehouse. We took quite a hit over the Christmas period due to Covid.

"Warehouse" is a bit of an overstatement—we simply cleared out the ground floor of the empty house we bought. The problem is that it's freezing in there, the windows don't shut properly, and there are dozens of swallows' nests along the beams. The swallows will be back soon, and we also need to start the renovation. I've already found a solution. There's another empty house opposite the bookshop, and the owners have agreed to let me use the large room on the ground floor as a warehouse. The house is stunning, very elegant, with a wonderful stone balcony. I've been asking the three owners for years what they plan on doing with it. They don't know. And so the house sits there, a shadow of its former self, where two very smart sisters from Lucca used to spend their summers when I was little. Norma and Darma would sit on the low wall outside the house or on the balcony in their heels and pearls, enjoying the cool breeze from the river. As soon as the construction begins, we'll move the books there.

In all this, I am still torn about something—what to do with the swallows' nests wedged between the ceiling and the beams? What if a little swallow is already on its way from Africa, headed home to one of those nests? A home we'll destroy? What if a swallow, having traveled more than 11,000 kilometers, averaging 320 kilometers a day, having flown over Nigeria and Morocco, past the Sahara Desert and Gibraltar, were to swing east across the Pyrenees and finally arrive in Lucignana, only to find its nest gone? I have to talk to Marco, our mayor, who used to be in charge of farming polices when he was a councillor. We have to find a way to relocate the nests. We have a month and a half.

—

Today's orders: *Cultivating the Mind of Love* by Thich Nhat Hanh, *English Country Houses* by Vita Sackville-West, *Farewell, Ghosts* by Nadia Terranova, *Il mondo deve sapere* by Michela Murgia, *All Things Cease to Appear* by Elizabeth Brundage, *Gulliver's Travels* by Jonathan Swift.

February 18, 2021

Love is in the air. One evening, while Giulia was packing her suitcase before heading back to Florence, I bumped into my great-nephew David and invited him in to say hello to my mother, his grandma. Fabio and David are the handsomest boys in the village, with Michele, our firefighting cherub, hot on their heels. Fabio's is a wholesome, reassuring kind of beauty, while David's is subtle and mysterious, ultimately lethal. In his eyes hide the ocean—if you fall in, you'd better be a good swimmer.

That evening, I felt I was being guided in a specific direction, playing a little part in a greater plan that was about to unfold. And I was right. Giulia and David barely exchanged a glance, seemingly ignoring each other. Then she asked him to help carry her suitcases to the car. Giulia is beautiful too—long black hair tumbling down her back, and very clever. Good swimmer. Two days later, David had moved in with her.

Yesterday Giulia phoned to tell me she wouldn't be working at the bookshop anymore because she wants to start her own business with David. She's not well, cries for no reason, and seems very confused. She's not the same girl I met in September. I heard talk of opening a bookshop in Palma de Mallorca—it sounds like a rash decision to me, but I said nothing. They're young and need to take risks.

I'm very worried about Covid, though. The Delta variant is extremely contagious, case rates and deaths remain stubbornly high, and the economy is on the brink of collapse. We're still in the "amber" tier, which is a real blow for us at the beginning of spring. I'll tend to the flowers, touch up the pergola, build a gravel path in the garden (the grass is too delicate to withstand the endless to-ing and fro-ing of visitors, and the result is a maddening, squelchy mess).

Donatella will lend a hand, of course. The bookshop helped her heal a wound—that's my theory, at least. She got pregnant at forty, unexpectedly. Another daughter. She told me one day as I bumped into her in Scimone—her eyes were shining so brightly. Sadly, the little girl never made it, and that was the beginning of a very difficult period for Donatella. I'm conceited enough to believe that helping me set up the bookshop—and she truly was invaluable—also helped her close that chapter of her life. Maybe she slotted it between a Kincaid and an Ernaux on a shelf and that, too, became another story, a story she could tell.

Donatella lifts crates of books like a trucker and scolds me when I'm late, which is very often. She owns a charming house, the same house Auntie Ange, my mother's eldest sister, used to live in. From her garden you can see the Sant'Ansano hermitage and behind it the Apuan Alps—the perfect backdrop for our summer *aperitivi*. Graziano got her a blue Adirondack deck chair, although she was opposed to the idea initially. She feels rather strongly about the bookshop having truly unique pieces, and another deck chair like that in Lucignana was not "appropriate."

Auntie Ange's daughter, Dora, also used to live in that house. Like Emily Brontë, she died of tuberculosis at thirty. Mama still has a photo of her, black-and-white obviously—dark hair coiled up in a bun, soft features. So little remains of our past that Dora's photo is to me like a whole family tree, marriages and children unfurling along the delicate curves of her nose and lips. In every family, there are always those who don't get married, who leave no heirs: dead branches. Dora, too, would have been a dead branch, were it not for this photo, which instead ranks her among the legions of those who died young—near-mythical figures forever etched in our collective memory. I'm sure Graziano knows nothing about Dora, but I have a feeling that his blue deck chair among the roses and hydrangeas was very much appreciated.

—

Today's orders: *Un paese di temporali e di primule* by Pier Paolo Pasolini, *Un prato in pendio* by Pierluigi Cappello, *A Woman's Story* by Annie Ernaux, *All Passion Spent* by Vita Sackville-West, *La scrittrice abita qui* by Sandra Petrignani, *The Last Thing He Wanted* by Joan Didion, *Diary of a Bookseller* by Shaun Bythell.

February 19, 2021

We hadn't had a winter so true to its name in years. It's been so gray and rainy. I checked the forecast on my phone, and it looks like we're in for a long spell of good weather, starting from next Sunday.

The garden's in a sorry state; I can't stand the sight of it any longer. I'll call the gardener, since I can't call one of my favorite writers,

Pia Pera, anymore. I still read her books, though, and I've embraced her "anti-gardening" stance. I won't be pulling out the wildflowers that grow behind the fence, like I stupidly did last year. Pia, who taught Russian literature, translated Pushkin's *Eugene Onegin* (among others), and rewrote Nabokov's classic from Lolita's perspective (*Lo's Diary*). She also decided to leave Milan and move back to Vaccoli, near Lucca, where she was born. She'd frequently clash with the farmers on her estate—over the killing of grass snakes, for instance, which they'd club before her very eyes, while she defended the crucial role "pests" played in the ecosystem. Defender of weeds and grass snakes, Pia was a true nonconformist in everything she did.

Once, I invited her to write a short text against the death penalty, and that's how we met. I remember her questioning gaze: Who was I? A member of the literati or a commoner? Friend or foe? Could I be trusted? She couldn't quite get the measure of me. For my part, I put her in the "friend" box straightaway, although I didn't get to prove it to her.

Death has a way of pulling the rug from underneath our feet, taking from us what we'd only just started. Pia began to limp, and after a few years, on July 26, 2016, she died, falling from her wheelchair down a little slope in her garden. A garden that, incidentally, was blissfully unaware of motor neuron disease. The garden hadn't been informed. Pia, however, with superhuman strength, had been writing a book, a diary of her illness. She had picked up Virginia Woolf's cane and wielded it as a scepter, pointing out the leeks and asparagus that were ripe for the picking. Then the cane wasn't enough anymore, and neither was her laptop or her phone. The superhuman strength of this woodland nymph had been worn down in the end, as had we. Her memoir is named after a poem by Emily Dickinson: *Al giardino ancora non l'ho detto* (I Haven't Told My Garden Yet). You will always find it in my bookshop alongside everything else she wrote.

Pia had bought a little house in Tereglio, which she'd found with Giovanna's help. One day I went looking for it with Pierpaolo—it wasn't hard to spot. Small, white, tiny windows, tiny pergola, tiny garden paths, and tiny doors. You could see her in every detail. It should be preserved. Maybe I'll go and check on it today. Pia is our Emily Dickinson—we can't let that place, her place, be sold, or altered, or destroyed.

Emanuele Trevi's latest novel, *Due vite* (Two Lives), is about her. They'd been friends for years. It's been longlisted for the Strega Prize—fingers crossed. As for me, I've been studying Pia's *L'orto di un perdigiorno* (An Idler's Garden) as a sort of spiritual preparation to tend to my own garden.

—

Today's orders: *The Rose Garden* and *The Springs of Affection* by Maeve Brennan, *Walking* by Henry David Thoreau, *The Overstory* by Richard Powers, *Drive Your Plow over the Bones of the Dead* by Olga Tokarczuk, *Sembrava bellezza* by Teresa Ciabatti.

February 20, 2021

For a month now I've been spending my nights here, in this room on the fourth floor of the stone house I inherited from my aunts. It feels like a tower, which makes me think of Montaigne and Hölderlin, and the role houses play in an author's life.

Towers especially. Towers isolate: in them, authors feel protected and secluded, disconnected from the world. Leaving the lowlands for the mountains, as it were, Hölderlin spent the last thirty-six years of his life in a tower by the Neckar River in Tübingen, the guest of a carpenter named Ernst Zimmer. Incidentally, a carpenter taking in a schizophrenic poet for thirty-six years is in and of itself a work of art. As for Montaigne, he simply retreated to his family castle a hundred kilometers from Bordeaux, between Castillon and Bergerac. He also had a tower waiting for him.

And a tower saved my life too—or at least that's what it felt like in that attic, in the house with the makeshift staircase. The house I'd been banished to after my brother's wedding, the house my father abandoned, and with it his wife and daughter, one night in 1972. The house with no bathroom, no heating, and a mother devastated by pain.

I fled as soon as I could, picking a school that strangely enough I could attend only as a boarder, in Florence. To this day I will never forget looking it up in the phone book, crammed in a phone booth with my father. *J, K, ...* There it was! Liceo Linguistico, on Via Ghibellina. It was a private school, but my father assured me he could cover the fees. The school recommended a boardinghouse run by nuns where I could stay. And that was that. I turned up in a pleated orange miniskirt my mother had made for me, which did not comply with regulations. I bought a longer tartan skirt, soon abandoned in favor of the de facto uniform students chose to wear at the time: jeans, parka, beret, and boots.

I'd go back home every Saturday to endless fights with my mother, enraged by the fact that I still got to see my father and she couldn't. Forty years went by—years of hatred and pain. Then, one day, my mother met Ming, a girl from the States who volunteered for a charity for elderly people in Florence—my mother was assigned to her. They grew extremely fond of each other, way beyond the weekly hour they were scheduled to spend together—I would even say they needed each other. In her soft voice, Ming would speak to Mama about forgiveness. And one day Mama said she would like to forgive Dad.

When she turned a hundred, the whole village got together to celebrate her birthday. We gathered at the Circolo della Croce Verde, mayor included, sash and all. My mother walked in, looking very elegant, accompanied by my brother. I led the celebrations, so I had a mic. I asked if anyone would like to say a few words. A man got up, handsome and smartly dressed, and slowly made his way towards the birthday girl, his arm stretched out towards her. As my mother, awestruck, got up, his hand tenderly slid in between her face and neck. The man kissed her and walked away; then he started crying. That man was my father.

—

Today's orders: *Drive Your Plow over the Bones of the Dead* by Olga Tokarczuk, *L'istante largo* by Sara Fruner, *White Fang* by Jack London, *The Handmaid's Tale* by Margaret Atwood, *Loving Frank* by Nancy Horan, *Learning to Talk to Plants* by Marta Orriols.

February 21, 2021

Today Alessandra made a traditional peasant dish from our region—chestnut-flour fritters with ricotta cheese. Here's the recipe:

Ingredients:
- 200g chestnut flour
- 250ml hot water
- 30g pine nuts
- Salt and baking powder to taste
- peanut oil
- 200g ricotta cheese

Method:

Whisk all ingredients together (except for the cheese and the oil) to make the batter. Ladle out in small quantities and fry in peanut oil. Once cooked, fill with fresh ricotta cheese, ideally from the Garfagnana region.

For centuries, chestnuts filled many a poor man's belly around these parts. The flour was ground from smoke-dried chestnuts kept in huts we call *metati*. Chestnuts could also be boiled (*ballotte*) or fire-roasted on a perforated pan (*bruciate* or *mondine*). To make the chestnut flatbreads we call *necci*, you mix chestnut flour with water and then spoon the mix into a pair of round cast-iron pans with long handles, greased with olive oil and heated on a woodstove— flip once and the bread is ready. In the old days, however, this was a more complex operation. People would use *testi*, terra-cotta disks, which would be heated up by the fireplace and then laid out on a wooden plank. Each *testo* would be lined with chestnut leaves (which were picked in early summer and then stored in tall piles, kept in place by a long thread run through the leaves with a needle). You'd then ladle the mix onto the hot disk, top with more leaves, and place another hot disk on top, leaving it to cook for a few minutes. It was a complete, nutritious meal, especially if you were lucky enough to stuff the flatbreads with ricotta or the blood sausage we call *biroldo*. A horticulture professor once told me that the tastiest, most flavorsome chestnut variety is known as *lucignanina*.

I like being a good host for our visitors. I'd love to serve chestnut fritters with ricotta, but Covid is still rampaging through the world. Today we're open, but only to the people in town. Not exactly a wild ride.

—

Today's orders: *Der englische Botaniker* by Nicole C. Vosseler, *Niente caffè per Spinoza* by Alice Cappagli, *Memorie di una contadina* by Lev Tolstoy and T. A. Kuzminskaja, *Tōkyō tutto l'anno* by Laura Imai Messina, *Mujeres que compran flores* by Vanessa Montfort, *Gli estivi* by Luca Ricci, *Autumn* by Ali Smith.

February 26, 2021

I've been in Florence for a few days. I owed them to Laura, who all of a sudden found herself motherless and running the house while studying for her final high school exams. We're always happy when we reunite and hold each other tight, but she's not alone, thankfully—she has Joy (her Italian-Belgian friend), Mirto (the wolf pup), and a little bunny. We decided to sell the house in Florence, which is too big now, and buy a smaller, more functional flat for her (besides, I could use some savings in these uncertain times). And to think that there was a time when Laura begged me to find a job that would allow us to live in Lucignana! I didn't seize the opportunity, and now it's too late; she's determined to stay in Florence. She'll feel that way again, with time. I for one cannot wait to be back—such is the irresistible power of places, of homecomings, of childhood. Such is the power of Monte Prato Fiorito.

Monte Prato Fiorito ("flowery meadow" in Italian), just north of Bagni di Lucca, is quite unique—made up of two rounded domes about thirteen hundred meters high, it is completely devoid of trees. These domes are a familiar sight for our bookshop visitors, and indeed for anyone in Lucignana. When I was little, I thought they looked like a big pair of breasts, soft and reassuring. In the spring they are carpeted in jonquils and are truly magnificent. If you make it to the top on a clear day you can see the Mediterranean—there are no crags or cliffs; everything's soft and round. Legend has it that the witches of Ponte del Diavolo (Devil's Bridge) would go up there some nights—including on June 24, the Feast of Saint John—and dance around a bonfire. As for me, I was jealous of those round, shapely domes—they reminded me that my own boobs just wouldn't grow. Some Sundays, I'd go to mass (the height of social life in the village) with tissues stuffed in my bra—push-ups hadn't made it to Lucignana yet. As a matter of fact, the domes are two separate mountains, Monte Prato Fiorito and Monte Coronato, but nobody here cares about these technicalities—only foreigners and tourists.

Sunsets on Prato Fiorito are magical. When everything around them has already been swallowed by the shadows, the two summits shimmer in the dying light as if under a spotlight while the sun sinks behind the Apuan Alps. These mountains have played an important part in my decision to come back and open the bookshop. From my house on Vicolo Sopra la Penna, I turn right onto a narrow gravel path squeezed between old walls, then right again at the end of the path, and there, before me, stand the domes of Monte Prato Fiorito. This view never ceases to amaze me. It's like a long exhalation after holding your breath all your life, the same feeling of exhilaration I experience when I run to the top floor of my tower house and step outside onto the balcony: the air, the stars, the sky, the whole wide world. *"E mi sovvien l'eterno,"* as Leopardi wrote. I am reminded of eternity. Horizons expand; lungs stretch out to the full; anxieties crumble in an instant.

A little over a year ago, as we were all gathered in the vicarage after mass, enjoying Alessandra's doughnuts, I opened my iPad and some photos of Lucignana popped up. Everyone rushed to take a look, hunching over me as if they'd never seen the village before, as if it were some exotic location like the Seychelles or Fiji. Tiziana, in particular, was thrilled:

"Where's that?"

"And that?"

"I mean, look at that!"

"The view from Sant'Ansano," "The view from Via Piana," "Virginia and William's house."

Yet they were all born here. Lived here all their lives. It makes me laugh when people say Lucignana is a "ghost town"—quite the opposite, I assure you. That's why I had to do something.

Yesterday I came back from Florence to an immaculate house—Alessandra had really outdone herself, like a little girl eager to impress her mother. Everything is spick-and-span, as I told Pierpaolo, who had to stay in Florence nursing a backache. Meanwhile, Maurizio (Barbara's husband) has started laying the flagstones for the garden path, and today, finally, we'll get a visit from the gardener.

I've just received a book that Pia Pera mentioned, and that I absolutely had to get my hands on: *Derek Jarman's Garden*, written by the celebrated filmmaker before he died of AIDS aged fifty-two. The garden in question is the one Jarman built on the desolate expanse of shingle that faces the Dungeness nuclear power station in England. I like books that make you discover other books—a virtuous cycle that should never be broken. The only eternity we will ever experience is here on earth, Pia maintained. Gardens are a slice of that eternity.

—

Today's orders: *Compulsion* by Meyer Levin, *The Museum of Innocence* by Orhan Pamuk, *Tu, paesaggio dell'infanzia* by Alba Donati, *The Way Through the Woods* by Long Litt Woon, *Tales of the Pacific* by Jack London, *Noi* by Paolo Di Stefano.

March

March 1, 2021

Yesterday was a sunny Sunday, and the bookshop looked resplendent. The garden patiently awaits another visit from its gardener, who should be back next weekend.

The pandemic, meanwhile, keeps killing us, both literally and metaphorically. March will be a tough month. Public health directives are now imposed on a council (rather than regional) basis—we're in a so-called white area, with the lowest level of restrictions, but we still can't have visitors from outside our council area. And so we wait— for a vaccine, for "salvation." One day we'll know—and by "we" I mean humanity as a whole—if we deserve to be saved, or if the world has grown too weary of our abuse.

I'd invited Dad over for lunch, and we ended up eating as in the old days, when we were a family. He seemed happy to be around people. In the afternoon he sat on one of the deck chairs in the garden and chatted to Graziano the whole time. I've been trying so hard to find him a place here in Lucignana, somewhere comfortable with no stairs, but no luck so far.

Mama wouldn't stop kissing us both, because every kiss could be her last. I can picture my dad, aged thirteen, dangling from the bars of a window, looking at a beautiful girl feeding her son, cheese and bread laid out on the table. He had nothing. There were too many mouths to feed at home, and his father struggled. The girl would pity him and let him in, sharing what food she had. But Rolando was insatiable—he'd have eaten the table, too, if she'd let him.

The girl was twenty-five and she was waiting for her husband to come back from Russia. She and little Giuliano kept waiting, hoping against hope. Rolando, meanwhile, had moved to Lucca, where he worked as a valet for a wealthy family. He learned to read and write from the newspaper he'd buy for his *signore* every day. He experienced a different world, which was all it took to reawaken his thirst for knowledge, the desire to make it in life.

At twenty-seven, he came back to Lucignana and asked that girl to marry him—the husband had never returned, and there was no hope left. And so it was that my mother married my father, a man twelve years her junior. My aunts protested, but then a beautiful baby girl arrived to mend all the tears.

When Dad came back from the garden, he was cold. As he sat down on the sofa, Mama wrapped his hands in a blanket and placed them on her lap—as if he were still that hungry boy at her window. I don't know if this miracle is my doing, or if I'm only playing a little part in it, but it doesn't really matter.

Two women came to the bookshop today, a mother and daughter from Tereglio. The books they chose are so wonderful, they made my day. The mother is called Natalia and owns the small grocer's shop in the village.

—

Today's orders: *All Things Cease to Appear* by Elizabeth Brundage, *The House in Paris* by Elizabeth Bowen, *Close Range* by Annie Proulx, *Una sostanza sottile* by Franco Cordelli.

March 4, 2021

We're expecting the gardener today. Last week's visit was just to inspect the site; now he'll get down to work. I bought some clover seeds to scatter in between the flagstones Maurizio laid down (the garden path, incidentally, looks really good, even the tricky bit by the gate).

Natalie wrote from Israel, the stockings are ready. Everything's perfect, in short, except for Covid, which continues to sow panic and poverty. We're looking at another month in lockdown—case rates are rising; schools remain closed.

Yesterday I took Dad to have his first dose of vaccine. He says he's absolutely fine, bless him, with his disability pension and everything. He really is something else. Dad supported me financially while I was still at university; then he got roped into some dodgy deal by his lawyer. In those days I'd do anything to get by and pay the rent, including selling dubious cleaning products door to door. An equally dubious company would arrange to have us ferried around in a minivan, me and other young girls who desperately needed money, and drop each of us at a different location somewhere between Lucca and Pistoia. We'd lug big duffel bags full of cheap detergents along endless roads, and then they'd pick us up and drive us back into town. My hands would get so stiff in the cold, frozen, as if on the Russian steppe.

Then I landed a job in a boutique in the city center—Sandro P., which in the eighties was considered the temple of fashion in Florence. I was twenty-eight. Sandro is a very genial character. Every now and again Vivienne Westwood would drop by—they were friends. She would sail in in her oversized coat and sit in a corner to warm up. The great Vivienne Westwood. She looked like she might be from Lucignana. Another frequent visitor, who most definitely did not look like he was from Lucignana, was Boy George.

But it was a tough year. Shop assistants had to be on their feet for eight hours, and I struggled. On my lunch break I'd go see a Polish-American friend (who I suspect was a little bit in love with me) and cry. She'd attempt to console me with some awkward caresses, which were gratefully received.

It reminded me that when I was a child, all the other kids hacked the grass with a scythe to make hay, filling their wicker baskets and going back and forth between the fields and the huts where the animals were kept. I'd just sit under a tree reading *Oliver Twist*. But Dickens couldn't save me in that shop—I couldn't sit down. Only Vivienne Westwood could.

I also organized a couple of themed events in a club that was very popular in those days—the Manila, just outside Florence. The parties were inspired by *Alice's Adventures in Wonderland* and *Vladimir Ilyich Lenin* by Vladimir Mayakovsky. I recruited some Alice look-alikes, my Polish-American friend made the costumes, and her boyfriend took some pictures in locations inspired by the books. We hunted down disused factories, crumbling walls, busted beds, old upholstered chairs. It was phenomenal work, and all for a little club in the suburbs. I must find those photos and hang them in the bookshop. Those girls must be fifty by now; God knows where they are. I could track down only two—Elena and Veronica.

—

Today's orders: *Cosí allegre senza nessun motivo* by Rossana Campo, *The Enchanted April* by Elizabeth von Arnim, *Qualcosa* by Chiara Gamberale, *Fried Green Tomatoes at the Whistle Stop Cafe* by Fannie Flagg.

March 5, 2021

The gardener managed to patch up the grass, which was disappearing slowly under a layer of mud. We sowed some clover along the garden path—I can already see myself inspecting it every morning, rejoicing in each millimeter of new growth.

On Facebook, I found dozens of posts about the bookshop by various visitors (mostly women). Giulia, a few days ago: "Know that you have gifted me a moment of not insignificant happiness. Keep up the good work." Adam: "Heaven is a place on earth. And it's called Garfagnana." Caterina: "Just leave me here." The other day, as she was leaving the bookshop, a girl paused by the sage-green gate, by the steps, by the flowers and the lanterns, and said: "Let me experience this moment. I've been dreaming of these steps."

The garden more than played its part in this. After we pruned it, the old tree that used to grow tiny, wrinkly peaches now produces the most spectacular fruit, and the leadwort bush gained a couple of meters in height. I've ordered an essential book on the power of flowers. It's called *The Intelligence of Flowers*, by the Belgian Nobel laureate Maurice Maeterlinck, and its beauty lies in the absence of any scientific or classificatory intent. Like us, Maeterlinck writes, flowers look for the easiest path, avoid the difficult ones, and fight: they possess a revolutionary spirit. Maeterlinck narrates the lives of flowers as if they were epic undertakings, at times doomed to fail. Take lucerne, for instance, whose seeds are enclosed in a light, spiral-shaped fruit designed to be blown far by the wind—but alas, it is all for nothing. Lucerne stalks are too low, and the seeds drop to the ground in no time.

Once, I saw a little boy running towards the bookshop and then stopping at the gate, in awe: "Wow, this is paradise!"

Derek Jarman reminds us that the word "paradise" comes from ancient Persian, originally meaning "luxuriant garden." His own garden at Prospect Cottage is luxuriant, and shaggy, and so is ours. If your "garden isn't shaggy," says Jarman, "forget it."

I don't know that our gardener reads Pia Pera or Derek Jarman, but I'm sure he agrees with them. He turned up armed with fertilizer and garden tools that wouldn't be out of place in a museum. Shaggy and proud.

—

Today's orders: *The House in Paris* by Elizabeth Bowen, *Mille anni che sto qui* by Mariolina Venezia, *Compulsion* by Meyer Levin, *Men Without Women* by Haruki Murakami, *The Autobiography of My Mother* by Jamaica Kincaid.

March 7, 2021

Our shop hours are fairly irregular. We're open every weekend, and last summer (our first summer) we were open Thursday to Sunday. Despite the mandatory booking system, every Thursday you'd see dozens of people who didn't manage to secure a spot queueing along the street. That's why this year, Covid permitting, we'll be open all week (but I'll take Tuesdays off; otherwise I won't be able to cope).

A few visitors came yesterday, and that brightened our mood. Andrea, the mayor of Castelnuovo, popped in too, together with the president of the Giovanni Pascoli Foundation, which seems to be up to all manner of good things lately. They asked if I'd be interested in becoming the foundation's artistic director—this could be a fruitful alliance. Just imagine: the fantasy epics of Ludovico Ariosto and Pascoli's poetic genius joining forces with a twenty-first-century microbookshop.

The more I think of it, the more I'm convinced Pascoli was a giant. He was horribly misrepresented by literary critics. All they saw was boring, decadent nineteenth-century mannerism—there was no mention of psychoanalysis (which in fairness hadn't been invented yet), nothing on Pascoli's innovative themes such as the harsh reality of immigration or the centrality of nature and animals, not a word on his experimental use of language (which Pasolini then chose as the subject of his dissertation). I think I'll accept, even though I certainly don't have time to spare right now.

Today we launched a little initiative on social media—a game of sorts, inspired by *Stai zitta* (Shut Up!), the latest book by Michela Murgia, where, with poignant sarcasm, she analyzes ten sentences women are fed up of hearing. The game consists of posting photos of women from Lucignana posing with the book and a finger pressed against their lips, as if to say, *Shush!* We aim to post one every four hours, including names and job titles in the caption, to celebrate International Women's Day. You should have seen the ladies of Lucignana hurrying home to change or put on some makeup!

The first to pose for her portrait was my mother. Occupation: centenarian.

I've heard every single one of those sentences myself, from "You'll scare all the men away!" to "It was only a compliment!" Come to think of it, I've heard way more, including "You're so old-fashioned!" (said by a married man after I'd turned him down) and of course the classic "You're so tense; why don't you let go a little, get rid of your inhibitions?"

We're still taking photos today, mainly of those who didn't want to pose yesterday because they had to get dolled up.

—

Today's orders: *Our Souls at Night* by Kent Haruf, *Christmas Days* by Jeanette Winterson, *Midsummer Night in the Workhouse* by Diana Athill, *Longbourn* by Jo Baker, *The Mitford Girls: The Biography* *of an Extraordinary Family* by Mary S. Lovell, *All Things Cease to Appear* by Elizabeth Brundage, *Little* by Edward Carey.

March 11, 2021

I spent another three days in Florence, which only strengthened my resolve: I don't want to live in a city anymore. I could see only the negatives—the grime, the noise, the traffic. The only positive note was my daughter and her nine-month-old gangly wolf pup, some sort of cross between Elvis Presley and the Pink Panther.

Last night, glancing at my refrigerator, I noticed an excess of butter and eggs and decided to bake an impromptu cake—weighing without scales, like Colette. Three eggs, flour, sugar, a pinch of baking powder, a chunk of butter melted in a dash of warm milk, thirty minutes in the oven, and hey presto, we have a cake. It was delicious. I was proud of myself: I'd proved I could cook in pinches, chunks, and dashes, which is the secret ingredient all literary critics rave about, that creativity, that instinct you cannot teach, categorize, regulate. "A dash of olive oil" defies analysis. George Steiner, Colette, Virginia Woolf, Elsa Morante: they all knew that literature is built on a dash of olive oil.

Where does that precision come from—Colette wondered about her mother's cooking—the confidence, the instinctive knowledge of people who barely ever leave their town?

In *Preoccupations*, Seamus Heaney confessed that in his first years as a lecturer in Belfast he'd produced some technically advanced verses, but devoid of the kind of preverbal energy that is the origin of all poetry. He wrote a lot but said nothing. Lifeless literary exercises. It was only when he let a certain word toss and tumble in his mind that the magic began. *Omphalos*—ancient Greek for "navel," or "the center of the world." Heaney would repeat the word in his mind—*omphalos, omphalos, omphalos*—"until its blunt and falling music" became "the music of somebody pumping water at the pump outside our back door." The source of all poetry lies underground. It predates language. Only if we can dig deep, where style cannot reach, will our words speak our childhood, our father, the landscape, the history of our nation. Robert Frost said:

> A poem begins as a lump in the throat, a sense of wrong, a homesickness, a lovesickness.

I wanted to bake that cake again today, but I was out of eggs. I'll get some tomorrow.

I traveled back from Florence by train, dutifully muzzled behind my Jane Austen mask. Donatella picked me up from the train station in Ghivizzano—I was tired and anxious, and her enthusiasm put me back together. We stopped at our favorite café, De Servi, and enjoyed hot chocolate topped with whipped cream—sitting outside, of course.

More targeted lockdowns have been announced. To avoid "large gatherings" (yet another ugly phrase that has entered our vocabulary), the government decided to ban travel and household mixing during weekends and holidays, including Easter and the early May holiday. A disaster for the economy.

Yesterday, in her consummate tragic tone, my mother announced to me over the phone that she belonged with "the living dead." I'm sure she meant that she's alive but might as well be dead, yet the choice of words rather implied the puzzlement of someone who, knowing full well they are dead, still finds they are displaying all vital signs. My mother is insufferable, but I suspect my flair for the dramatic must come from her.

Natalie wrote from Israel: our stockings were dispatched on March 3 and should be here by March 28 (in theory). Fingers crossed, they'll arrive in time for Easter, for our online shop at least.

—

Today's orders: *Complete Poems of Emily Dickinson* and *Letters of Emily Dickinson* by Emily Dickinson, *Mrs. Dalloway* by Virginia Woolf, *Hotel Bella Vista* by Colette, *The House in Paris* by Elizabeth Bowen, *Umami* by Laia Jufresa.

March 12, 2021

It's raining—faintly, but still raining—good news for my little clover seeds buried in the garden.

Yesterday Donatella and I went to Fornaci di Barga. She was in a hurry—her cousins Barbara (Maurizio's Barbara) and Tiziana are unwell, and she was given a detailed shopping list for each. I watched her leap out of the car under the rain and dart through the crowd with her tiny umbrella, avoiding puddles. In her cashmere bonnet with a dainty bow and her gray ankle-length coat she looked like someone straight out of a novel, say Holly Golightly from *Breakfast at Tiffany's*, hopping out of the car like a gazelle, like Audrey Hepburn hopped out of her cab on Fifth Avenue.

Then she came back, laden with bags, beaming. Nothing seems to bother her; she walks through life as if through a dream. Except for the bookshop, that is, which she takes extremely seriously.

Yesterday two girls came from Valdarno—they had booked their visit and taken a day off work to come to the bookshop. Readers after my own heart, who pick books I love and prick up their ears if they see me take something from a shelf. Readers who leave with big smiles behind their masks and will definitely be back.

They bought *An Unnecessary Woman* by Rabih Alameddine and *Cuore cavo* by Viola Di Grado, two novels published several years ago that we filed under "evergreen." I really enjoy scouring the Web for "outdated" books to rediscover. One thing I noticed as a bookseller is that "cult authors" are not really a thing. There aren't *that* many people waiting for Paul Auster's or Zadie Smith's next novel—there are many more who will never forget a novel whose author they cannot remember. People want stories. It doesn't matter who wrote them; they need stories to take their mind off things, stories to identify with or to take them elsewhere. Stories that won't hurt, that will heal a wound, restore trust, instill beauty in their hearts.

When customers ask me what a book is about, I'm at a loss. I've never remembered a plot in my entire life, not even "Snow White and the Seven Dwarfs." I retain other things, which to me are the essence of literature. Authors, I believe, are forever at war with plots, their core message fighting its way through plot lines to lodge itself inside the reader's heart. I know, for instance, that in all the books I choose there is always pain, some kind of defeat. So what do I say to those who ask for a "painless" book? The covers come to my rescue—reassuring, romantic, with a dash of irony. Dashes and handfuls again. "This book grabs me," said a girl once, of a book lying flat on a shelf. Evidently, that book had a dash of what it took to be taken home. It was *Breakfast at Tiffany's* by Truman Capote.

—

Today's orders: *The Tree* by Steve Marsh, *Around the World in Eighty Days* by Jules Verne, *Le cose così come sono* by Silvia Vecchini, *Annie:*

Il vento in tasca by Roberta Balestrucci Fancellu, *Prince of Thieves:
Tales of Robin Hood* by Alexandre Dumas.

March 14, 2021

Winter's back. It's very windy and temperatures will dip below
zero Celsius. In a calculated act of defiance, our plum tree looks
resplendent in its cloud of pink blossoms, some of which have fallen
on the ground, forming a soft carpet at its feet, picture-perfect in
the sparkling sunlight. I'm hoping that, after this icy week, spring
will be here to stay.

Donatella and I opened the bookshop today but closed it shortly
afterwards, disheartened by the cold. We had a dozen people in
yesterday, all from nearby villages: Ghivizzano, Calavorno, Piano
di Coreglia. We're still able to travel only within our council area.

There was a girl—miniskirt, cropped coat, no tights, five-inch
heels—who took lots of selfies. That's clearly what she came for:
she needed a charming backdrop. Her friend, at least, was interested
in the books.

We need to be patient now, wait for the vaccines to kick in and
the case rates to drop. By then it'll be May, people will be itching
to travel, and visitors will flock to the bookshop. From all over Italy.
Like last year.

Angelica dropped by today, gliding down the steps, her feet
barely touching the ground—a butterfly. Those legs of hers are made
for leaping into the air, not walking. Her mother, Barbara (Daniele's
Barbara), came in too.

An interesting character—a smart cookie, as Daniele described
her once. She studied engineering but then quit just before grad-
uating. She's one of those women who dress to blend into the

background, never want to be in any photos, and buy only sober, functional furniture. But there's one detail that offsets this extreme minimalism—her voice. Books could be written about the infinite modulations of her voice and the effect they produce on people. To paraphrase a popular Italian advert from the 1960s, "With a voice like that, you can say whatever you want." It reminds me of Kathleen Turner's Jessica Rabbit.

Barbara bought *Eventide* by Kent Haruf and *Il mare dove non si tocca* by Fabio Genovesi. Angelica wanted "a grown-up book." She considered several options, including *Oliver Twist*, but then chose *Maffin* by Massimo De Nardo (which looks like a grown-up book but is targeted at a YA audience). It's about a boy who has to build a clock that can never go forward or back. A nice story.

—

Today's orders: *La Claire fontaine* by David Bosc, *Lourdes* by Rosa Matteucci, *Die Lieben meiner Mutter* by Peter Schneider, *Wat er van het leven overblijft: Een damesroman* by Sigrid Combüchen, *L'olmo grande* by Gian Mario Villalta.

March 15, 2021

A wonderfully bright day. It is seven o'clock in the morning and my tower is bathed in sunlight. The tower has an en suite bathroom too, and from the shower I can see the mountains and the sky. I feel so grateful sometimes—as a survivor, someone who has somehow made it, despite it all.

The house, the house again, that blasted house. Aside from the makeshift staircase, there was something else—a source of deep shame as well as fear. There was no bathroom. None of the houses in Lucignana had a bathroom in the 1960s, but then they all built one. Except for us. Dad left, and left us bathroomless. My mother, to spite him, left everything as it was—"Why don't *you* build one? Why don't you ask *your father?*" As a result, we still used the old "seat," built in stone directly above the cesspit. And where, you might ask, was this architectural wonder of centuries past? At the very back of the bottom basement. A huge windowless room stacked full of logs, with a rickety door that barely closed. To get there you had to go outside and cross a little underground passage. I was six years old. My brother had married, my father had left, and my mother was incapable of demonstrating affection.

Later, when my school friends from Florence would come to visit for the weekend, I'd mutter warnings and explanations. Oh, the shame. "If that's your loo, it means nobody loves you." And it means you've had to battle dragons and snakes, dark nights, and all manner of terrors.

After years of agony, I knocked on my therapist Lucia's door. "Doctor, I dreamed that my mother was roasting a beef joint. Except it wasn't beef; it was me. Newborn me." "Doctor, I dreamed that it was snowing and I heard something rustling in the garden. I went out and started digging in the spot where I could hear the noise. There was a little girl buried in ice. It was me." Lucia looked at me with her discerning blue eyes, and immediately understood we'd be seeing a lot of each other in the coming years. Twelve years, to be precise.

After years of working as a governess, by the early 1990s Auntie Feny had saved enough money to refurbish her house, and, seeing as Auntie Polda had died, we moved in with her on Vicolo Sopra la Penna. There was a bathroom. With a shower. The refurbishment had completely obliterated some great original features, but it didn't matter—the house had all mod cons and that was enough. That's the same property I refurbished myself, by stealth, two years ago—I kept Mama in Florence for six months and completely changed the layout of the house (which in the meantime we'd inherited from Auntie Feny). Mama still pines for the old kitchen, the old living room—everybody tells her it looks fantastic now, but she liked it better the way it was. She has her reasons, of course, as I have mine.

—

Today's orders: *L'acqua del lago non è mai dolce* by Giulia Caminito, *Stai zitta* by Michela Murgia, *Il bosco del confine* by Federica Manzon, *Storia della mia ansia* by Daria Bignardi.

March 16, 2021

Today was spent trying to knock some sense into my mother. Alessandra, Monica, Donatella, and I argued that talking incessantly about coffins or how to dress her for her funeral (apparently the appropriate outfit must include black rosary beads around the deceased's neck) is rather counterproductive, as is constantly bemoaning every aspect of her life. Because she doesn't lead a bad life, as we all pointed out. Quite the contrary. She is almost 102, and while she might have lost her sight, she can still get around on her own and has no ailments to speak of. She lives in a beautiful house with her daughter (me), who is always around, and lots of people come in to see her every day. So why the daily panic attacks? It makes no sense. Ernesto, in all this, hit the nail on the head: "You're right, of course, but I'm here, holding her tight: that's what she needs, and I give it to her."

If by 3:00 p.m. Ernesto isn't here, Mama will go over to his house and ring the bell. He'll come in, sit next to her, and chat. He's learned to listen to her too. He listens to her pain without trying to understand it. At 6:00 p.m. he turns on the TV and blasts out a litany of Hail Marys live from Lourdes. At 6:30 he kisses her "tiny little head" and leaves. Every single day. No, it's not an Almodóvar film. No, he's not a devout Christian.

Time for some rose-hip tea and homemade biscuits from Luisa.

—

Today's orders: *Drive Your Plow over the Bones of the Dead* by Olga Tokarczuk, *Old Possum's Book of Practical Cats* by T. S. Eliot, *Virginia* by Emmanuelle Favier, *La notte si avvicina* by Loredana Lipperini.

March 17, 2021

I've posted the last of today's orders and now I don't know what to do with myself. I've browsed some books, examined the ground looking for clover shoots. It'll be a tough couple of months without visitors climbing up our street to get to the bookshop. Our country, the whole world, in fact, is a bunker. Lucignana, for its part, remains Covid-free, which adds to the surreal atmosphere of the past few months.

Yesterday I started sending out invitations for an event I'm curating for the Giovanni Pascoli Foundation. Melania G. Mazzucco, Michela Murgia, Emanuele Trevi, Fabio Genovesi—they all RSVPed yes, Covid permitting. And then there's Toni. When your day starts with a phone call with Toni Servillo, you've already won. Once, as we were having dinner in Florence after an event dedicated to the late Cesare Garboli, Toni scooped me up from a table—the table I'd fainted on, that is, landing right on my dining companions—and took me outside. Emanuele Trevi was there too. That was the second time I'd fainted during a dinner with Emanuele—and I've fainted only twice in my entire life. Anyway, today I asked Toni to read Pascoli's poem "Italy" on August 10 in Casa Pascoli, and he agreed. Not bad for a day's work. I should ask to be paid for stuff like this, so that I might finally repay what I owe my old supplier. Not that he's chasing me—no one's chasing, because no one has any money right now, and we're all just lucky to be alive.

Many have written to me asking how I did what I did, and how much it cost. It's hard to give a definitive answer, but what I do know is that you'll need at least €30,000 worth of stock to start. If you do what I did, which is order books and pay for them as you sell them, you won't make it. You'll always need more books but also struggle to sell many of the ones you already have, and if you don't keep track of your cash flow you'll end up in a right pickle. You need at least €30K, for your peace of mind. Oh, and keep an eye out for government grants; they can make a big difference.

As for our bookshop, we've learned that female authors sell really well.

—

Today's orders: *Scusate la polvere* by Elvira Seminara, *All Passion Spent* by Vita Sackville-West, *Tōkyō tutto l'anno* by Laura Imai Messina, *The Green Wiccan Herbal* by Silja, *L'Italia di Dante* by Giulio Ferroni.

March 18, 2021

The weather forecast no longer shows snow, low temperatures, and strong winds for today. Maicol, however, still chases after the wind:

"But where is it? Where?" he asks his grandmother, who keeps telling him it's too windy to play outside.

Maicol's story, and that of his mother, Sandy, is truly heart-breaking. Sandy has always looked after her twin brothers as if they were her children. She didn't really get to be a child herself, or a teenager. One day, she met a guy she fell madly in love with. His name was Massimiliano and he adored Sandy, but he'd just lost his job and was trying to stay afloat. He owned a little house in a nearby village, but it was too small for Sandy's family to live in. Then she got pregnant and they planned to move in together, just the two of them. One night, however, Massimiliano fell ill—high temperature, couldn't breathe. An ambulance took him to the nearest hospital, where he was immediately admitted to the ICU. Sandy never saw him again—after a month he was dead. This was March 2019, Covid hadn't entered the picture yet, and no one could explain his death. Maicol looks exactly like his father. And despite everything, he is a very happy boy, eager to learn, switched on, bright. He was predicted to be an "anomaly"; instead, he is the heart and soul of the family. That's life. He was told that his daddy is up there in the sky, on a big cloud. Maicol seems happy to know he's there, and smiles his cheeky smile. Once, as they were eating in the garden, ready to pounce on a plate of spaghetti, Maicol stood up and, looking very serious, pressed a finger to his lips: "Shush!"

"What's wrong, Maicol?" asked his mother.

"Daddy's here," he replied, pointing at a cloud printed on the tablecloth. "Ssshhh!"

—

Today's orders: *La grammatica dei profumi* by Giorgia Martone, *Vegetables: A Biography* by Evelyne Bloch-Dano, *Un Appartement à Paris* by Guillaume Musso, *L'acqua del lago non è mai dolce* by

Giulia Caminito, *Il bosco del confine* by Federica Manzon, *Thirst* by Amélie Nothomb.

March 19, 2021

Today is Father's Day in Italy, and this morning a bank of clouds drifted over Lucignana, as if all the village's lost fathers had gathered to spy on the living from the comfort of their misty homes, to see if they're still loved. But the sky's clear now, and everything's immersed in a peaceful silence. Sandy posted a photo of Maicol sitting on a step, looking intently at a flowerpot. He knows his daddy is nearby, because on the tablecloth there are flowers around the clouds. So he keeps a careful watch—Daddy, his daddy, could be just around the corner.

As for me, I have to be wary of what's around the corner these days—I seem to have acquired a hater. This is what an ex-journalist from a big publishing group, who recently relocated back to Florence from Milan, wrote about me a week ago:

> The esteemed poet Alba Donati, muse of Lucignana, poor man's Gertrude Stein, honorable member of feminist cabals, with literary accolades and friends in high places bestowing upon her an overdose of credibility . . .

And what had I done to earn such a rebuke? I'd replied to a Facebook post by a friend of mine at the center of a media spat, saying that you really can't call a woman a cow, not even a fascist woman, especially not on the radio. The portrait this ex-journalist painted of me is textbook misogyny. A mud-slinging, vitriolic, chauvinistic character assassination. I was particularly struck by the comparison with Gertrude Stein. He could have said Virginia Woolf, Karen Blixen—but he chose Stein. Maybe he got mixed up. Maybe he meant George Sand, who kept wonderful herbaria in her country estate in Nohant. That would have been more accurate, because I do share her fixation with flowers and gardens, and her childlike excitement. Like Maicol, I, too, look at flowerpots, waiting for something magical to happen. I, too, like Sand, listen to *ce que disent les fleurs*, what flowers say. You can say whatever you want, dear hater, but this is for real. I'm for real.

In the first page of his memoir, Shaun Bythell warns his readers that he rather fits the stereotype of the "impatient, intolerant, anti-social" bookseller à la Dylan Moran in *Black Books*. And quoting Orwell ("Would I like to be a bookseller *de métier*? On the whole . . . no"), he admits to having legions of haters on social media.

Well, I'm not like that. I'm not impatient, intolerant, and anti-social. I'm curious, cheerful, positive. I peer into customers' bags to see what they've bought, make tea for everyone. I like to see the good in people. Heightened confrontations such as the one I got dragged into throw me into a rather unbalanced state. Vanity is the worst of sins. And spending hours contemplating a flowerpot to see if it's all right, if it needs anything, if it wants to talk—like Maicol, like George Sand in Nohant—is the one thing that puts my soul back where it needs to be.

—

Today's orders: *Qualcosa* by Chiara Gamberale, *Les Villes de papier* by Dominique Fortier, *Rosa candida* by Auður Ava Ólafsdóttir.

March 22, 2021

It's 6:00 a.m. The weekend netted us a grand total of eight visitors, plus splendid sunshine and arctic temperatures. Luckily, online orders are keeping us afloat.

Donatella couldn't come, as she was busy organizing a sale of children's shoes. Years ago she'd opened a little boutique with her daughter, far too fancy for where we live. The shop's long gone, but they still have some stock in their basement, and they sell it off little by little to mobs of mothers and aunts rooting through the piles of shoes, looking for the right size and color. But Donatella's as tough as they come, pretty unflappable.

Yesterday we exchanged a few messages—I sent her a picture of a haircut that I think would look great on her. Donatella married "a foreigner," which is to say a guy she met in a club thirty-five years ago. Graziano is one of those old-fashioned, earnest men—unabashedly possessive when it comes to Donatella, but clever enough to accept the resulting mockery with good grace. The truth is, as Ernesto is very fond of saying, that Graziano is still on his honeymoon. And he's right—you won't find a couple more madly in love than those two.

Donatella is two years younger than me, an age gap that felt unbridgeable when we were little. Childhood is the proof that time is entirely subjective. When I was thirteen, Donatella's uncle came to visit from Australia with his son, Silvano, who was eighteen. That was a phenomenal summer. We spent hours dancing to rock 'n' roll in my basement. I contributed our cassette player, he his Elvis Presley tapes. You should have seen his moves—John Travolta and Uma Thurman in *Pulp Fiction* had nothing on us, gyrating in a basement along with all the "little ones": Donatella, Luana, and Tiziana. Silvano was smitten; I was flattered. I wore miniskirts and I'd started to develop something resembling curves.

Anyway, the summer of '73 was a memorable one. It was bookended by the inauguration of the World Trade Center on April 4—which left me largely indifferent—and another event that instead resonated deep inside my young bones: Pinochet's coup in Chile and Allende's suicide on September 11. As for us, we kept dancing, without a care in the world, in our basement ballroom. The following year Silvano came back, convinced he had a girlfriend in Lucignana, but I had moved to Florence. For this Donatella never forgave me.

Today is Monday, which means Alessandra will be here shortly. I smile, anticipating our usual conversation:

"I'd like my breakfast, please."

"Would you, now? How about some coffee and a nice 'fuck you' to start the day?"

I adore her. Later we'll go to check if Mike's house has been damaged by last night's storm. I only wish our stockings from Israel were here—that'd be perfect.

—

Today's orders: *Apprendista di felicità* by Pia Pera, *Childhood, Boyhood, Youth* by Lev Tolstoy, *Why the Child Is Cooking in the Polenta* by Aglaja Veteranyi, *Can't Wait to Get to Heaven* by Fannie Flagg, *Peter Pan* by J. M. Barrie.

March 23, 2021

This morning at seven o'clock I went to Piazzolo to witness the desolation around Lucignana's little parking lot. They cut down all the trees: lime trees, chestnuts, spruce trees, acacias. When I asked why, I was told that "there was an injunction signed by the council" and that "the trees belonged to the diocese anyway." That's the drastic approach they adopted to mitigate the risks the trees posed to parked cars. Why research, prune, protect, when you can just cut down? When it comes to environmental protection and the preservation of beauty, it's always one step forward and two steps back.

I took a couple of photos, picked up some kindling for my fireplace, then came back home. I was thinking of the days immediately before we opened the bookshop, when Tina Guiducci came from Milan and we brainstormed categories and sections, stuck labels on shelves, and positioned signs. Tina doesn't belong to my previous life or, strictly speaking, in my current one (the bookshop, that is)—she's some sort of continuous presence, as if she'd always been around. I'd known her by name for several years; then one day, at the Mantua Literature Festival, I saw her whiz past on her bike in blue jeans and a crisp white shirt, understated and radiant in the September sun. I don't know how we became close, but we did.

I remember seeing a beautiful woman in the garden last summer— we were wearing the same colors. She told me she was Tina's mother.

"I'm so glad you're friends with my Tina," she said. "I brought you a plant."

I know there must be a deeper meaning behind her words, but I didn't inquire. I water that plant every day and that's that.

One weekend last year, Tina took part in our "Bookseller for a Day" initiative, which I intend to revive as soon as Covid relents. She was amazing: hypnotized, the visitors bought all the books she recommended. I remember this elderly lady, a retired Italian literature teacher who'd sat down on a chair in the middle of the bookshop. She quizzed Tina for more than an hour—a true clash of the titans. I can't help but think that we should put Tina in charge of our trees. She would know how to avoid mutilating our streets, our houses, our walls. She would know what to do. That woman can do anything if she puts her mind to it.

No sign of the stockings yet. I'm hoping at least the paint I've ordered will turn up, so I can paint the sun loungers. I'm taking care of you, my beloved garden, little by little, waiting for someone to sit down, for flowers to be sniffed and pages to be turned, for tea to be sipped. Waiting for questions, for eyes softening into a smile.

—

Today's orders: *Pride and Prejudice* by Jane Austen, *Before the Coffee Gets Cold* by Toshikazu Kawaguchi, *Hotel Bella Vista* by Colette, *Occidente per principianti* by Nicola Lagioia.

March 26, 2021

It's been a hectic week. My mother grows more demanding by the day; someone in Laura's class tested positive for the dreaded Delta variant (queue jumping through endless bureaucratic hoops to book a PCR test); I've got books coming in, books going out, and a father who needs ferrying to his vaccine appointment. Luckily, my beloved clover has finally sprouted all around the garden path, which is extremely satisfying.

By seven o'clock I was already in the garden, inspecting the new growth. You need to talk to the green shoots, like George Sand would do as a little girl, and perhaps as a grown-up too. Clover needs awakening from its subterranean slumber, violets reassuring they won't be trodden on, peonies reprimanding for their laziness (not a single bloom last year, but I can already see some red buds now—good sign).

I cannot get over the desolation at Piazzolo. Those solitary stumps, an emblem of man's folly. I'd like to hang a copy of Peter Wohlleben's *The Hidden Life of Trees* on every felled trunk. I will, in fact. A "land art" installation.

Dad told me those trees had been planted by him and other

primary school children: each tree represented a soldier who'd lost his life during the First World War. Bet they didn't know, those who ordered the trees to be felled. Maybe they never even saw the trees, just had them cut on a whim, to make their lives easier.

There's a little chapel dedicated to the Virgin Mary where people would go to pray or find shelter. It's just outside Lucignana (hence the name Marginetta—"on the margins"), two hundred meters from Donatella's house, at the end of a path lined with spruce trees on the way to the Sant'Ansano hermitage. Despite the damaged cobblestones, it made for a very pretty view: a chorus of fir trees leading to a dainty little church. No more. The firs are gone. No one can justify this decision. And I, for one, won't accept it.

—

Today's orders: *Bottled Goods* by Sophie van Llewyn, *La gioia dei vagare senza meta* by Roberto Carvelli, *Italian Life* by Tim Parks, *A Home at the End of the World* by Michael Cunningham, *Absolutely Nothing: Storie e sparizioni nei deserti americani* by Giorgio Vasta and Ramak Fazel, *Senza polvere senza peso* by Mariangela Gualtieri.

March 27, 2021

Good news: the stockings are finally here and already available on our online shop. With a caveat: they can be purchased only alongside a book (and our readers, it seems, are all too glad to be thus blackmailed). Speaking of which, I've decided who my "ideal reader" is. Her name is Raffaella and she lives in Milan—I don't know her, and although she's been following us for some time now, she's never actually been to the bookshop. I find her curious, perceptive, unconventional, and elegant. Yesterday she messaged us a photo of Peter Schneider's *Die Lieben meiner Mutter*.

Good morning, I've looked but I can't see it on your website.

Oh, it's not available yet.

I see—can I add it to my order?

Of course.

Thank you, I always ask, but I also trust your recommendations.

I hope it's working out for you!

Oh yes, and by the way I love how you showcase new books on your Instagram stories.

(I send her some photos of the new Jane Austen socks, in white and beige.)

Oh, I've just realized I've run out of Bottled Goods *by Sophie van Llewyn, would you like me to reorder it? Or would you prefer to swap with something else?*

Any recommendations?

Let me get back to you.

Sure, no rush.

(I send her photos of *La Petite conformiste* by Ingrid Seyman, *Valentine* by Elizabeth Wetmore, *A Tree Grows in Brooklyn* by Betty Smith, *Learning to Talk to Plants* by Marta Orriols, and *L'istante largo* by Sara Fruner.)

I knew it—I like all of these. Impossible to choose!

I swear I didn't do it on purpose.

Today's Saturday, and as of Monday we'll be back in tier "red"— full-blown lockdown. Easter's just around the corner. I'll work on my land art installation, make roasts and soups, and wait for Laura's PCR test results.

—

Today's orders: *La Petite conformiste* by Ingrid Seyman, *Valentine* by Elizabeth Wetmore, *A Tree Grows in Brooklyn* by Betty Smith, *Learning to Talk to Plants* by Marta Orriols, *The Better Sister* by Alafair Burke, *Les Villes de papier* by Dominique Fortier.

March 28, 2021

I don't seem to be able to fully enjoy my days lately—as if I'd only just realized that we are in the middle of a pandemic, that our lives have changed, that fear and uncertainty weigh on us all. Those who worked in the arts sector have lost everything; many have gone back to their little towns (the lucky ones who had little towns to go back to).

Nobody's going to starve here in Lucignana. Adriana brings us eggs, Francesca marinated anchovies and potatoes, Tiziana scallops and fritters (plus some baked goods from our beloved De Servi café), Donatella her mother's minestrone—and there's no shortage of firewood over at the cemetery of the felled trees. More than enough to go around. Yesterday Donatella brought me two bunches of ruby-red tulips. That's Lucignana for you, our sharing culture. The village is one big home—its streets corridors, its houses rooms. Maybe I survived my childhood because I did have a home after all.

Tomorrow is Palm Sunday and we'll be open. We had three visitors today, all after our new stockings and socks. As of Monday, however, no more bookshop for a week; we'll hunker down and bake biscuits. We're still waiting for Laura's PCR test results—she's coming over for Easter with Mirto, aka the Elvis of the canine race, and maybe even her bunny. It'll be cozy for sure.

I can't wait to get my hands on Max Porter's latest novel, *Lanny*. A boy, a village, plants, clearings, bark, and flowers—green magic. Like Orwell, like Lethem, like Bythell, Porter has worked as a bookseller—and that's all I need to know.

I'm guessing *Lanny* could be to my 2021 what *Ordesa* by Manuel Vilas was to my 2020. A book that, despite focusing on Vilas's parents' death, truly sets you alight with life. When I think of Vilas's father, I see my own. The white linen suits, the dignity in the face of financial ruin. One sold fabric across Spain; the other built houses. It was the seventies, and both men had been the first in their families to start their own business. If I ever meet Vilas, I'll tell him how they destroyed my father.

His mistake was not hiring an accountant (or, worse, thinking *I* could be his accountant). He did everything himself—up and down various building sites all day with his fourteen employees, then slouching over quotes and invoices in the evening at the living room table. A tough life. And when he came across some nasty characters who refused to pay, it was even tougher. Days spent begging for what he was owed, unanswered calls, burning humiliations. Poor Dad, he was so honest, and he wouldn't hurt a fly. And so it was, my dear Manuel, that he ended up owing a lot of money to the banks. But he still had an ace up his sleeve—he owned a large industrial warehouse on the main road to Lucca, which would have been perfect as a showroom. He'd had some interest from a car dealer who was ready to pay 450 million lire for it, the equivalent of a million euros today. But (there is always a "but") Dad's lawyer took it upon himself to inform the potential buyers that if they waited a few days they could snap up that same property at an auction. Such a lovely man, wasn't he, Manuel? And wait they did.

But—once again—it didn't end there. The lawyer summoned my father to his office to formalize his demise (everything he owned would be sold at an auction the following day), and that's when the trap closed in. He told my father he'd found a company that could help him: they'd be paying off his debt in exchange for all his assets, which at the time were valued at just under 2 billion lire (4 million euros in today's money). Once the debt had been cleared and the assets sold off, they would be sharing with my father whatever money was left.

I'm not even sure Dad understood what he was getting himself into, but he signed. The company was called S.U.A. *Sua* is Italian for "his," and it was indeed his—the lawyer's, that is. Needless to say, the contract made no mention whatsoever of any "profit sharing" after the sale. And that, my dear Manuel, is how Dad, in his white linen suit, lost everything. It hurts to see defeat in your father's eyes. But we got some revenge: we sued two of his creditors, the two who'd humiliated him most, and won. Not the lawyer, though—he died with his money, his villa full of expensive art, and trace amounts of guilt. In all this, Manuel and I still profited: just like his own, my father's misfortunes provided endless narrative fodder.

—

Today's orders: *The Rose Garden* and *The Springs of Affection* by Maeve Brennan, *Cortile Nostalgia* by Giuseppina Torregrossa, *Questo giorno che incombe* by Antonella Lattanzi, *Blue Nights* by Joan Didion, *Dear Life* by Alice Munro.

March 29, 2021

Yesterday it was just me at the bookshop, the sun was shining, and although I didn't expect anyone, a few people turned up. It's a well-known paradox that the closer you live to something, the less convenient it becomes to visit. If it's far enough away, however, you can make a trip of it, a fun day out, an experience. I still remember how we laughed when a girl phoned to ask about the course the veteran literary translator Tim Parks was holding at the Fenysia School of Languages and Cultures. The course was aimed at literary translators from Italian into English, and dozens had signed up from all over Europe and even the United States. Hearing that the course would be held in Florence, the girl commented that it was too far for her (she lived in Livorno, less than two hours away). Time and space really are just illusions.

The bookshop is no exception: we had more visitors from Sicily and Trentino than from Calavorno or Ghivizzano, four kilometers away. The pandemic, however, flushed out even the most reluctant neighbors, and every now and again they do drop in. Yesterday Sandy brought Maicol in for the first time. I like the idea that children should see Lucignana as a place where—as well as running, riding a bike, and playing hide-and-seek—you can find crocodiles, rhinos, mice, cats, dinosaurs, pirates, and princesses. We also learned that Noemi is expecting a boy, so with Maicol, Diego, and Samuele that's 4–0 for the boys. We're still waiting to hear about Fabio and Federica's baby, though.

This week I'll be working on my proposal for the playground and submitting it to the council. I want to make sure we'll have at least a climbing frame with a slide, a couple of swings, and a skipping rope by May. Also on my to-do list is painting the sun loungers and the round armchair—I got some teal paint to match the bookshop's palette.

Grass and flowers are growing nicely in the garden, while the tree stumps by the chapel just stand there, lonely as can be. The saddest thing, however, is that nobody cares. In *Ordesa*, Vilas writes:

We come from the trees, the rivers, the fields, the cliffs.
Our world has always been barn, poverty, stink . . . If God
or whoever offered us paradise, within four days, with you
and me in there, we'd turn it into a pigsty.

Well, not everyone, actually—there are a few enlightened souls, like Lanny.

—

Today's orders: *Gli anni al contrario* by Nadia Terranova, *Lady Susan* by Jane Austen, *House of Splendid Isolation* by Edna O'Brien, *La bambina che somigliava alle cose scomparse* by Sergio Claudio Perroni.

March 30, 2021

They're here. Yesterday I saw three in the main square—I looked up and there they were, looking tired but glad to be home. *Chirrrr . . .*

chirrr . . . chirrup. I listened to their chitter-chatter as they looked for their street, for the exact address. And on Vicolo Sopra la Penna, where the work is yet to begin, their little homes still clung to the beams; in they flew with a jubilant shrill. I shut the door, the better to spy on them: the nests were all aflutter with confabulating, incessant deliberating—a quarrel, perhaps? I learned the word "onomatopoeia" studying Pascoli's poetry in school. An ugly term for such a beautiful concept. I prefer "mimetic harmony." And when it comes to mimetic harmony, Pascoli was second to none. His swallows sound like a flash of the unexpected. They speak as we humans would, if we could voice that note of eternal youth.

We had some wonderful orders yesterday. Incredible how social media can motivate readers—we've noticed that, generally, they're quiet when we're quiet, but if we post a picture of a gift-wrapped book, the orders start coming in thick and fast. Social media has effectively replaced daily editorial meetings. These days, you have to post every morning, you have to get that message out: "If you're looking for something new to read, a nice present for a loved one or for yourself, look no further! Libreria Sopra la Penna has you covered—now with added swallows!" (You can't ask for a better testimonial than that.)

I've painted the sun loungers, the grass is growing, the peach tree is blossoming, the temperatures shot up to 26°C yesterday and I put on my blue muslin dress and trusty (fuchsia) Birkenstocks. I had a call with the mayor of Florence and Tommaso, a friend of mine who is now the culture secretary for the Florence city council. Main point on the agenda: funding cuts to the Vieusseux Scientific and Literary Foundation, of which I am president. They were so stressed, bless them. White as a sheet. I worry about them—they are young and take everything so personally. I used to be like that too; now I choose not to be. I'm a real girl now, like Pinocchio (I never could make up my mind if I liked Pinocchio better before or after his transformation).

I've always admired Edward Carey, and we ended up becoming friends. He is a fantastic author and illustrator—I immediately fell for his gloomy, Dickensian atmospheres and post-Gothic yet extremely delicate graphics. Two years ago, I suggested he rewrite *Pinocchio*, a story he often mentioned. With his usual enthusiasm, he dived right in—into the belly of the shark that swallowed Geppetto, that is, to see how the old carpenter spent his days all alone in the dark. In Carey's hands, *Pinocchio* turned into a survival guide, a fairy tale about our memories and their ability to keep us alive. The project was first presented as an exhibition for the Collodi Foundation (somberly curated by Valeria, the same Valeria who designed our bookshop).

As always, Sergio Claudio Perroni's translation was spot-on. Edward is a wordsmith, or a word baker, rather: someone who mixes and kneads scraps of old words to make new ones. Sergio is his Italian voice. Take the Iremonger trilogy, for instance, which should be required reading for all ages: *Heap House, Foulsham, Lungdon*. Consider the subtext of "Lungdon," which Sergio translated as "Lombra." Edward Carey wrote:

> *Londra* is the Italian word for London, and he titled the book *Lombra* which, while nodding to the city perfectly, is also the Italian word for shadow. That is pure Perroni, confident, dark and pitch-perfect. Changing a word but illuminating it, making an exact connection between my English and his Italian.

Edward's *Pinocchio* was then published in the UK as *The Swallowed Man*, with endorsements from Margaret Atwood and, as chance would have it, Max Porter. Talk about mimetic harmony. Harmony that is nothing short of magic, harmony that—like the swallows—whirls and twirls and follows its own path.

After all this talk of harmony, I really need Alessandra to re-balance things a bit—our friendly, sweary neighborhood thug, a cigarette forever dangling from her lips. Say what you want, but if she's not around to, say, change the toner in my printer like she did yesterday, I simply cannot function.

—

Today's orders: *The Complete Poems* by Emily Dickinson, *Le Peintre d'éventail* by Hubert Haddad, *The Door* by Magda Szabó, *What Happens at Night* by Peter Cameron, *All Things Cease to Appear* by Elizabeth Brundage, *Dai tuoi occhi solamente* by Francesca Diotallevi, *Fried Green Tomatoes at the Whistle Stop Cafe* by Fannie Flagg.

April

Yesterday I got a message from Vivian Lamarque: "I'm reading your beautiful poem 'Camminavo sotto i platani' in the wonderfully ponderous *La poesia degli alberi* collection."

And again: "I love that line—'With that "U" all on its lonesome.'"

And finally: "Did you know, your *platani* are right next to Paul Valéry. And in alphabetical order, D for *Donati* comes right before E for *erba* and F for *fiori*. Plane trees, grass, and flowers: a forest in a book!"

Oh, to have the gift of irony and levity, like Vivian! That quintessentially female irony that with a trifle, a comma, can subvert entire hierarchies. Oh, to have penned the wonderful "A vacanza conclusa":

We are poets.
Admire us while we live
Not after we've died
As we won't be around to notice

Italian readers had got used to Eugenio Montale's brand of irony—detached, disengaged. This is something else. Take Wisława Szymborska, to many Italian critics just an old lady with an unpronounceable name, until she was awarded the Nobel Prize and people started paying attention. The irresistible irony of these lines from "Under One Small Star":

My apologies to the felled tree for the table's four legs.
My apologies to great questions for small answers.

A sweet melody calling out to us to switch our perspective, even as we are, like all humans, lost in a crowd of other humans—jumbled sticks, tangled threads. And if we're lucky, someone will pick up our thread—someone who was in turn saved from the snarl of life—and ever so gently pull us out. It's a delicate operation: one wrong move, a slightly thoughtless remark, and it's over. I'm far from pitch-perfect myself. I can't do irony, for starters.

—

Today's orders: *The Rose Garden* and *The Springs of Affection* by Maeve Brennan, *Cortile Nostalgia* by Giuseppina Torregrossa, *Questo giorno che incombe* by Antonella Lattanzi, *If This Is a Man* by Primo Levi, *Il cuore non si vede* by Chiara Valerio.

April 2, 2021

The PCR test came back negative. Laura is coming tomorrow with Mirto and Peaches the bunny—a burst of joy and chaos for our house. Lucignana, it appears, is still holding out—no Fascist Party cards and no Covid. For now.

Yesterday I switched things around at the bookshop. Seeing as we seem to sell mostly female authors, which according to some is my fault for relegating male authors to the lower shelves (and thus, as Alberto Manguel would argue, making them invisible to visitors, who only ever see what's right in front of them), I positioned male authors side by side with their female counterparts. In all this, the big loser was travel literature, now eclipsed on the bottom shelves—but I know its loyal fans will always seek it out, no matter how inconveniently located. Let's see what happens.

For now, all this painting and repotting and switching things around is to me like a meditation exercise. It reminds me of the meticulous care with which, as a child, I'd prepare lessons for my imaginary class in the attic at the top of the makeshift staircase. I would lay out a dozen old notebooks, and armed with a red pencil and an eraser I'd mark my own homework and comment on the grades. That game was so real to me that to this day I can picture every detail, down to the school desks that were most definitely not there. That attic full of old coats, tiny spiders, and a collection of various bits and bobs my mother was storing for God knows what eventuality was my kingdom. That's where my friends and I "played Sanremo," which is to say we pretended to be famous bands competing in Italy's popular music contest. Ricchi e Poveri was our favorite. There were Luisa and Anna (Lucignana's own mean girls), and then there was Alda, who like me would often be excluded on a whim.

We were very fond of each other and we did have a lot of fun, despite the inevitable meanness that scars all childhoods the world over. In our little game, Luisa would invariably claim the role of Angelo (Ricchi e Poveri's handsome lead singer) and I that of Marina (the blonde)—little Anna simply *had* to be the brunette (Angela), which meant that Alda was left with big-nosed Franco. Luisa and Anna had lush hair, worn in long braids—the envy of every little girl in the village. Alda, the chubby, good-natured one, was forever being picked on. She would be excluded from our games or from the group altogether, entirely at Luisa's and Anna's discretion—a fate that so often befell me too. Today we call it bullying, back then it was "kids will be kids," but the outcome remains the same: There was a victim. A little girl who suffered.

Alda ended up marrying young and had two children, Elena and Alessio. She died suddenly, sitting on the sofa watching TV next to her mother. She was only forty-two. I think of her often, and this is

Lucignana's real strength: one hundred and eighty souls plus Alda, Roberto, Paolo, Bruno, Maria Pia, Franca, Maria Grazia, Simonetta, and all the others. As Emanuele Trevi so deftly said:

> We live two lives, both destined to end: the first is our physical life, blood and breath; the second is the life we live in the minds of those who loved us. And when the last person we were close with also dies, well, that is when we truly dissolve.

A village, however, can preserve memories even longer, because our actions get snagged in the cobblestones, the fields, the woods. Dora, who died before I was born, still lives in Donatella's house; of this I am certain. And Alda is just around the corner, in a house full of children, just the way she liked it. And I'm sorry about the big-nosed guy from Ricchi e Poveri—I'll be Franco next time, I promise.

—

Today's orders: *Il giardino che vorrei* by Pia Pera, *Vita* by Melania G. Mazzucco, *Atlante degli abiti smessi* by Elvira Seminara, *Stai zitta* by Michela Murgia, *Mandami tanta vita* by Paolo Di Paolo, *Nightwood* by Djuna Barnes.

April 3, 2021

Yesterday, as I wrote, I fully realized the meaning of Emanuele's book *Due vite* (Two Lives)—maybe everyone else understood that straightaway, but to me it was a belated revelation. The two lives he talks about are not simply the lives of his late friends Pia Pera and Rocco Carbone, but also the second life we, the living, grant to our beloved who have passed away. They live on as memories. But it doesn't end there, Trevi argues. The dead are not passively summoned by our words—they have agency:

> Of this I am certain: as I write, and as long as I sit here writing, Pia is with me. . . . From this I evince that writing is a remarkably effective way to conjure the dead, and I would strongly advise anyone who finds themselves longing for a departed friend to do the same: not to think about them, that is, but to write about them. You will soon come to realise that the dead are irresistibly attracted to writing, and will always find unexpected ways to resurface in our words; but make no mistake, this is no apparition conjured by our memories—it is them, I'm telling you, in the flesh.

It is 8:00 a.m., and I must run outside to breathe in the crisp air from Monte Prato Fiorito, and check on my grass and peonies, and on my peach tree. I also have a box of new books to tend to, which never fails to bring me joy. Plenty to keep me occupied until Laura arrives.

—

Today's orders: *Gratitude* by Delphine de Vigan, *L'istante largo* by Sara Fruner, *The Consolations of the Forest: Alone in a Cabin on the Siberian Taiga* by Sylvain Tesson, *View with a Grain of Sand* by Wisława Szymborska.

April 4, 2021

Today, Easter Sunday, Dad joined us for lunch. In a matter of seconds, Mama went from her customary gloomy mutterings about the afterlife to a flutter of chirpy cheerfulness. She'd even put on a black velvet skirt, rather short for her, and looked very elegant.

We ate lasagna made by Luisa and her mother (who is a phenomenal cook), zucchini soufflé, and roast beef with roast potatoes. When Dad left, Mama turned to poor Ernesto (who might have even been a tad jealous) and said: "Isn't my husband a handsome man?" There were no further comments on the matter.

I spent the day chasing after Mirto, who darted out of the house as soon as an opening (literally any opening) presented itself, plowing furrows up and down Lucignana's streets with his keen young legs. Once, he almost made it into the church and I—sporting an ancient sweater and decidedly unfashionable hair clip—had to run the gauntlet of suits and blow-dries to retrieve the beast. Laura slept all day, before and after lunch. Last year she had a big hunk of a boyfriend who adored her. On the sad day Kiko left us, he dug a grave under the plum tree with such dedication that it was soon deep enough for him to disappear into, all six feet of him. He did everything—cooking, washing, ironing—but it couldn't last: he was all in, she'd barely dipped her toes in the water.

Anyway, today I didn't manage to read a single page. The afternoon took on a surreal, Almodóvaresque flavor that I couldn't shake off.

Scene: TV blasting out Hail Marys live from Lourdes.

Ernesto (shouting over the TV): "I got you some Easter bread!"

Mama: "Dead? Who's dead?"

I got up and joined Pierpaolo at Barbara and Maurizio's, where the impression of living in an Almodóvar film faded away as dusk crept slowly down the valley.

—

Today's orders: *Some Flowers* by Vita Sackville-West, *Pride and Prejudice* by Jane Austen, *The Secret Life of Trees* by Peter Wohlleben,

La Fille de Debussy by Damien Luce, *The Way Through the Woods* by Long Litt Woon.

April 5, 2021

> Hello, I just wanted to let you know that I've received your parcel, and it's such a surprise every time, because even though I've chosen the books myself—books you recommended—it's the care you can sense in the wrapping, the scent, the flowers and ribbons . . . it's all so wonderful, truly wonderful. I'm so happy I found you.

This was Raffaella from Milan, my "ideal reader," who buys books by the dozen and always asks for my recommendations while also following her own, unique taste. Every time she receives her order, she'll abandon our usual written messages and leave me a voice message in her plummy Milanese accent. I await them as eagerly as she awaits her books.

To paraphrase Orwell: Would I like to be a bookseller *de métier*? Yes, yes, I would like that very much. But maybe it wouldn't be the same without my garden, without Lucignana, Prato Fiorito, this silence. Maybe mine is a rather extreme bookselling experience— radical, idyllic, embedded in and living off this land, feeding on the paradox of its existence. A bookshop that, on paper, was destined to fail but ended up reaching out to and intercepting many kindred spirits, plucking them out of the storm and leading them safely home. A home that doesn't quite have everything, but most of what you need. That's why every day I get up at seven o'clock to open the bookshop, water the plants, tidy the shelves, and check on the peonies, knowing full well that no one will come because we're in lockdown.

I still do it, *regardless*, because something so radical and idyllic will not abide by ministerial decrees. Because passion cares nothing for success, and feeds on its own fire. "Why did you open a bookshop in a village in the middle of nowhere?" Because I needed to breathe, because I was an unhappy child, because I was a curious child, because I love my father, because the world's gone to the dogs, because readers cannot be abandoned, because we have to educate the new generations, because at fourteen I cried alone in front of the TV when Pier Paolo Pasolini was murdered, because I had wonderful teachers, because I survived.

Hello, I'm a woman—a wife, a mother. I turned forty in December. I've been working in healthcare since I was twenty-four, but I feel I don't belong here anymore, my job doesn't align with me anymore, it's not who I am, and for years now I've felt like I couldn't breathe. I'm dissatisfied, looking for my true calling and for the courage to make a change. This pandemic opened my eyes and spurred me to write to you and ask for advice. I don't know where to start, I'd like to open something like your bookshop, something that might also function as a cultural hub for our community, and maybe even more.

This message I received hits the nail on the head. One day you wake up and you're forty and you realize your "good job" isn't enough anymore. Maybe you tell yourself you'll wait until you retire to follow your passion—except by the time you retire your health isn't quite what it used to be. We've waited far too long to be who we want to be. In his tremendous *Cancer Ward*, Aleksandr Solzhenitsyn writes that if we constantly frustrate our true selves, those heart cells, created by nature to experience joy, will atrophy, unused.

This reminds me of Massimo Troisi in *I'm Starting from Three*, where he incites his friend Robertino to run away from his mother's house, which he calls the museum. We have to heed our folly, break free of museums, and remind ourselves that our cells were made for joy, not for retirement.

John Muir, who—alongside Emerson, Thoreau, and Aldo Leopold—was one of the founders of modern environmental ethics, listened to his heart cells when he abandoned his engineering career and embarked on a "flower pilgrimage" which, from Kentucky, would take him a thousand miles south to the Gulf of Mexico. He chose a life of wandering. To him we owe the existence of the great American national parks.

—

Today's orders: *Agathe* by Anne Cathrine Bomann, *The Dinner* by Herman Koch, *Del dirsi addio* by Marcello Fois, *Pariser Rechenschaft* by Thomas Mann, *Riviera* by Giorgio Ficara, *Marguerite* by Sandra Petrignani.

April 7, 2021

Mama's birthday is coming up; in eight days she will be 102 years old. Things aren't great between us—she's manipulative and stubborn as ever; I'm nervous and irritable. Thank goodness for our "village," especially Ernesto. His patience is akin to devotion.

Laura, Mirto, and Peaches have gone back to Florence. It was heartwarming seeing how much Mirto enjoyed being here—a ten-month-old wolf pup tearing through Lucignana like some sort of pagan deity, half dog, half eagle. And it was heartwarming seeing Laura, too—so grown-up, organized, caring, and positively stunning with her blue, almond-shaped eyes.

On the flip side, temperatures will drop again, it'll rain all week, we're still in lockdown, and businesses won't be allowed to reopen until after June 2. So upsetting.

Yesterday Donatella, Tiziana, and I went to the florist, where—hidden behind a rather flashy azalea—I found a mauve rose plant, my favorite color. I bought it. It's not easy to talk about flowers, as Vita Sackville-West reminds us—and she should know, seeing as she created one of literature's most famous gardens at her estate in Sissinghurst. She did, nonetheless, talk about them in a book called *Some Flowers*, where she describes and advises how to care for twenty-five flower species she particularly liked (painters' flowers, she maintains, rather than gardeners' flowers).

Sackville-West's prose is energetic and vibrant, free from all mannerisms. Describing the color of a flower without resorting to botanical banalities is no mean feat, but she pulls it off. Her reference point was the botanist Reginald Farrer, who had a special talent for discovering new flower species. In 1914, he traveled to China and Tibet with William Purdom, who had previously been on botanical expeditions to China. They brought back many plants previously unknown in Europe, such as *Gentiana*, *Viburnum*, *Clematis macropetala*, and *Daphne tangutica*. Many of these were later named after Farrer himself. None of his works were translated into Italian, which is a shame, but Sackville-West quotes his description of *Gentiana farreri* when he first saw it:

In no other plant [. . . .] do I know such a shattering acuteness of colour: it is like a clear sky soon after sunrise, shrill and translucent, as if it had a light inside. It literally burns on the alpine turf like an electric jewel, an incandescent turquoise.

And now my day, too, burns like an electric jewel: Tina called; she will be with me shortly. I must go to open the bookshop, make sure everything's perfect when she gets here. The sun is shining too— we're all set.

—

Today's orders: *Letters of Emily Dickinson* by Emily Dickinson, *My Name, a Living Memory* by Giorgio van Straten, *Last Things* by Jenny Offill, *La città interiore* by Mauro Covacich.

April 8, 2021

I've been rereading *The Door* by Magda Szabó, definitely in my personal top five of unmissable books.

It's the story of two women, Magda (the great Hungarian author herself) and Emerenc, her housekeeper. As solid and pragmatic as Magda is strong-willed, Emerenc is one of the most elaborate literary characters that ever existed, because she did, in fact, exist—this is a true story. It goes like this. On the day she's supposed to leave for Greece to receive a prestigious prize and represent Hungary at a literary conference, Magda Szabó decides on a drastic intervention: she must get through to Emerenc, who has been barricaded inside her own house for a month, since she first noticed the symptoms of an illness that prevented her from being herself, which is to say, a woman with the strength of six men. She refused to show the world her vulnerability. When people began to notice a nauseating smell coming from Emerenc's apartment, Magda knew she had to act fast. Pretending to be alone (when in fact she had arranged for a team of doctors to take Emerenc to the hospital), she convinced her housekeeper to open the door, and then, without even entering, she jumped in a taxi to the airport. The mother of all betrayals.

In October 1998, my first poetry collection won the Mondello Prize (in the debut category) and I went to Palermo to accept the prize. I remember getting the call from Vanni Scheiwiller, who'd published Eugenio Montale and Ezra Pound, at 7:30 in the morning. He was very complimentary, I couldn't believe it. Prizes in the other categories went to Javier Marías, Carlo Ginzburg, Philippe Jaccottet, and Pietro Marchesani for his translation of Wisława Szymborska's *View with a Grain of Sand*. I then ended up working as a publicist for the Mondello Prize, and was invited to attend all subsequent award ceremonies.

In October 2005, Magda Szabó won the Mondello herself, in the foreign-author category, for *The Door*. I remember this graceful, petite woman with eyes like a cat. Despite her advanced age, she arrived alone, visibly fatigued. And yet on the Saturday morning she still monopolized the press conference—she could not stop talking about her agonizing guilt, of how she betrayed Emerenc's trust. Incredible how such an exquisitely crafted book could spring from so excruciating a pain.

After the press conference, with the award ceremony about to begin, Magda disappeared. I had a sudden premonition and, with the hotel staff, rushed to her room. The door wouldn't open. Her suitcases were wedged against it. Like Emerenc, Magda had barricaded herself in her room. The firefighters and ambulance crew found her on her bed, seemingly unconscious. There was no one to look after her apart from me, so I sat next to her in the hospital as her Sicilian roommates attempted to cheer her up with various anecdotes delivered in a thick Palermo accent. Magda managed to give me the number of a relative, a nephew. I remember his thick mustache and penchant for beer. The diagnosis, meanwhile, had been delivered: transient ischemic attack, more commonly known as a "mini stroke," caused by fatigue and advanced age.

After that incident, Magda Szabó lived another two years, until November 19, 2007 (I kept in touch with the mustached nephew, asking after her health). *The Door* is now a film starring Helen Mirren as Emerenc.

Many claim it isn't a fully autobiographical novel. They're right; it's much more than that. It's an atonement novel. I still cannot get over the beauty of the scene where Magda visits Emerenc in the hospital and tells her all the lies she wants to hear: that her cats are all still in the house, that nobody went in and it was Magda's husband who fixed the door, that nobody saw and nobody knows about the excrement, the cockroaches, the rotting food. But it's all for nothing—Emerenc won't even look at her. Dejected, Magda is about to leave, and just as she turns and makes for the door she hears Emerenc whisper: "Magduska, my sweet little Magda." I cry every time I read it, like I cried when I held her hand in the hospital.

—

Today's orders: *The Light of Evening* by Edna O'Brien, *Alice's Adventures in Wonderland* by Lewis Carroll illustrated by Rébecca Dautremer, *Alice's Adventures in Wonderland* by Lewis Carroll illustrated by Helen Oxenbury, *Little* by Edward Carey.

April 9, 2021

Alessandra is my very own Emerenc, no doubt about that. Bossy but also very protective of me, there is something ancient in her.

Her gait has the steady cadence of centuries, the sound of undergrowth rustling under your feet. Alessandra used to live just outside Lucignana, in an area known as Maurilio's. The Maurilio in question was her father, who, just like Alessandra's brother Roberto now, was a sheep farmer. It's considered quite "eco chic" now, but in the 1970s, when we were little, Alessandra must have felt like an outcast, someone who had to go the extra mile to be accepted by our community. I can't help but think that, just like Emerenc with Magda, it was Alessandra who chose me, not the other way around. I had to sit through a job interview with her, as it were, and was hired as resident absent-minded, head-in-the-clouds writer. I quite like it up there in the clouds, to be honest: lots of interesting people to chat to, such as Massimiliano, who spends his days watching his son, Maicol, grow.

When I was little, I was convinced I could fly. I'd step on a rock and leap into the air, picturing myself gliding over Lucignana, which looked really beautiful from above. Donatella's mother would always be there, sweeping the road, like she did all her life. Just another job. I wondered why nobody else seemed to have got the knack of flying when all it took was a little bound to send you zigzagging through the blue like Wendy in *Peter Pan*. My favorite book was *Pippi Longstocking*, which is perhaps where my tendency to live alone, without boyfriends, originates: Pippi was so happy all by herself in Villekulla Cottage, with only her horse and her monkey for company. The book had a big orange hardback cover, and I also loved the film, which I'd watch at my uncle Fernando's. Come to think of it, that's not a million miles away from Laura either, living alone in that big house with her winged dog and Peaches the bunny.

We're hunkering down for a cold and rainy week, but then spring will come, and with it the vaccine, and with the vaccine the ability to travel, and everything will be (almost) perfect.

Today's orders: *The Woman in White* by Wilkie Collins, *The Violent Bear It Away* by Flannery O'Connor, *Incidents in the Rue Laugier* by Anita Brookner, *Die Lieben meiner Mutter* by Peter Schneider.

April 10, 2021

I'd forgotten how marvelous it is to be up here, on the top floor, at night, when it rains. It reminds me of a word I love: "shelter." The feeling of having escaped life on the streets and cheated poverty is very, very real here. As far as I'm concerned, Pascoli's long-lost "nest" has been found at last, and it is here, on the top floor of 7 Vicolo Sopra la Penna. Here shelter means happiness, pride, compassion. My dear auntie Feny, you didn't work all those years away from home for nothing—your niece has a home now, beautiful, warm, solid. I'm like a fourth little pig, the luckiest one, with the best of aunties.

I can hear the pattering of rain on the skylight and the stream gushing through the woods. I try to think of all the books and short stories about rain:

- *The Rain Before It Falls* by Jonathan Coe
- *The Rain Watcher* by Tatiana de Rosnay
- "Rain" by W. Somerset Maugham
- *History of the Rain* by Niall Williams
- *Kao ni furikakaru ame* by Natsuo Kirino
- *Henderson the Rain King* by Saul Bellow
- *Some Rain Must Fall* by Karl Ove Knausgård
- *Black Rain* by Georges Simenon
- *L'omino della pioggia* by Gianni Rodari and Nicoletta Costa

- *Cries in the Drizzle* by Yu Hua
- *La danza della pioggia* by Paolo Febbraro
- *La pioggia fa sul serio* by Francesco Guccini and Loriano Macchiavelli
- *Ilona Arrives with the Rain* by Álvaro Mutis
- "For Rain It Hath a Friendly Sound" by Diana Athill

That said, the most beautiful thing ever written about rain remains Gabriele D'Annunzio's poem "La pioggia nel pineto."

Yesterday Giulia called (our Giulia from Lucignana, not the one who is leaving for Palma with my great-nephew) to tell me that a group of fifteen girls would like to book a bachelorette party with us at the end of June. I live for stuff like this. Like Raffaella's orders. I've learned something new about her: her daughter, an eighteen-year-old eco warrior, is an Aries, whereas her father, who like me was a Cancer, passed away two years ago. I've just finished wrapping her latest order—books, compotes, lots of ribbons and flowers.

—

Today's orders: *What You Can See from Here* by Mariana Leky, *La bellezza dell'asino* by Pia Pera, *The Vegetarian* by Han Kang, *Edward Hopper* by Yves Bonnefoy, *Idda* by Michela Marzano, *Lila* by Marilynne Robinson.

April 11, 2021

Yesterday it rained all day, and the garden soaked up all that precious water to grow and prosper. In four days Mama will turn 102 and Marco, our mayor, will join us to celebrate. She will ask him two questions: first, if there's room for her at the nursing home in

Coreglia, which in local jargon is known as "the poor old people's home" (not that poor, mind you, considering the fees), and second, if he reckons her stomachache could be a sign her heart is failing.

The other day Don Giuseppe, our parish priest, came to visit. She chatted to him for half an hour, then asked if he knew whether the priest would turn up. She says she didn't notice the black robes— she did, however, notice he was handsome. My mother was always quite attuned to physical beauty. Years ago, even as she obsessively reminded Laura to eat, she'd spy her with her keen seamstress eye and declare to me, "She's put on weight, that's for sure."

Anyway, it's always such a joy to receive a visit from Don Giuseppe. His voice radiates protection, safety, and elegance. He's our priest, but also a surrogate husband, boyfriend, father. During his first mass, seeing as we couldn't shake hands as a sign of peace, he told us to blow each other a kiss, as you would to a loved one who's leaving on a train. Needless to say, we're all quite smitten with him Pierpaolo laughs, but I notice he's rereading Goffredo Parise's *Il prete bello* (The Handsome Priest). You never know.

I've been expanding our online catalogue—more books, but also more bookmarks, more pendants with literary quotes, and even masks with the silhouette of Jane Austen's leading characters—Elizabeth, Elinor, Marianne, Emma, Fanny, Anne. I've ordered more stationery too—notebooks with floral motifs, or inspired by Neruda's poems, or again by Ungaretti's "*M'illumino/d'immenso.*" I've reordered Natalie's stockings but heard nothing back, as per usual. I'm thinking of buying a small wrought-iron sofa for the garden to create a little cozy corner with cushions and quilted throws—all very romantic.

"Romantic" features quite a lot in our visitors' accounts of the bookshop, which pleases me. Romanticism was the first literary movement where women rose to prominence, from Madame de Staël to George Sand via the Brontë sisters, Mary Shelley, and

Elizabeth Barrett Browning. Nature was also a major theme across all Romantic authors, calling us to reevaluate our relationship with the natural world. A call we did not heed, and now here we are, revisiting Emerson, Thoreau, Whitman.

—

Today's orders: *La Petite conformiste* by Ingrid Seyman, *Nehmt mich bitte mit: Eine Weltreise per Anhalter* by Katharina von Arx, *Jane Austen at Home* by Lucy Worsley, *Il libro della gioia perpetua* by Emanuele Trevi, *Tōkyō tutto l'anno* by Laura Imai Messina, *The Bookshop* by Penelope Fitzgerald.

April 12, 2021

Yesterday Anna came in to bandage a wound Mama got falling down the stairs. Yes, that'll be Anna, the little bully in plaits, now a nurse and downright Lucignana institution. She never married, and had a daughter, Angela, who works in a supermarket. Anna's brother, Claudio, is Alessandra's husband—a village like ours is all one big family, really.

We laughed so much reminiscing about our childhood exploits. I remember our "expeditions" well. Three little explorers dressed like De Niro in *The Deer Hunter*, traipsing through the woods shouting, "Don't worry; I'll go first," except when we went to the hermitage, that is, and slipped inside the area that was closed to visitors, the hermit's house, as we called it; then we'd send Anna ahead, who, being the youngest, had to do as she was told. Alda was never there when I was—as always, the two sisters decided who was in and out of favor.

Then there were Johan Cruyff, Émerson Leão, and Franz Beckenbauer, respectively the Netherlands midfielder, Brazil's keeper, and West Germany's central defender during the 1974 World Cup, as well as mine, Luisa's, and Anna's "boyfriends." Seeing as mobile phones hadn't been invented yet, we'd send each other postcards: "Meet me in Gelsenkirchen at 7 p.m. Yours, Johan." Said postcards were invariably intercepted by our mothers, who genuinely believed we were sneaking out to meet boys in mysterious "Gelsenkirchen," and consequently grounded us for days.

As the years went by, my infatuations started ranging closer to home. I met another Anna, my very first best friend, with whom I shared my not-so-secret crushes on teachers and soap opera actors like Franco Gasparri. We wrote to each other a lot during the first two years I spent in Florence; then my interests slowly shifted towards feminism and Pasolini, and our paths began to diverge. Today Anna works for a charity helping disabled people to find their voice through theater—she doesn't need Pasolini for that.

We know so little about the future. Will I ever see our garden teeming with readers of all ages again? Will we die less and heal more? Will the vaccines work? Natalie is yet to answer my email, but the new stationery turned up—lots of flowery notebooks. We need flowers these days, more than ever.

—

Today's orders: *La bellezza sia con te* by Antonia Arslan, *L'acqua del lago non è mai dolce* by Giulia Caminito, *Some Flowers* by Vita Sackville-West, *La felicità degli altri* by Carmen Pellegrino.

April 13, 2021

Natalie replied. Apparently, it's some sort of national holiday in Israel, so we'll talk about the stockings next week. Meanwhile, Barbara

(Daniele's Barbara) and I added new books and accessories to our online shop—all things Jane Austen, Alice in Wonderland, Harry Potter, and Emily Dickinson. My new Frida Kahlo sun lounger turned up too—bold bright colors and the iconic painter's face staring at you from the canvas.

I ordered some new books, too—new to me, that is. I'd barely opened Niall Williams's *History of the Rain* when I got well and truly sucked in:

> The longer my father lived in this world, the more he knew there was another to come.

Williams's concept of "a second draft of Creation" is so captivating that it should be accepted as dogma: where God made mistakes, he ought to correct them. We all get a second chance, above all God, who invented second chances. He should focus on pain—not erase it altogether, but preserve a memory of it as a bump on the road, as it were, something that no longer exists, because in this second, "finer" Creation men and women will not "know despair." Pain as memory of pain. If he ever does get around to his second draft, dear Jesus, will you please tell your dad to look into this?

When I was little, I talked to Jesus every evening, addressing him more like a friend, a brother-in-mischief: "Will *you* please tell Dad I won't do that again?" I'm not sure what exactly I had to atone for; maybe not being Johan Cruyff's actual girlfriend, or excluding Alda, or perhaps the dreaded "sins of impurity"? This phrase I would always say quickly but say it nonetheless, because it was a neat little formula that encompassed all manner of things best left unspecified—a convenient expression to mask adolescence's many hormonal and sensory earthquakes.

Anyway, *History of the Rain* is a great book. *Lanny* I've put aside for now—I'll get back to it.

Yesterday I told Alessandra about Magda and Emerenc. She listened, her eyes fixed on mine. As it happens, yesterday Antonella Lattanzi, an author I admire, also wrote about *The Door*, calling it a seminal book. Jung called these coincidences synchronicities, postulating that the universe possessed its own form of intelligence, which generated harmonies. A universe that detects and brings together the elements it feels are seeking each other in the endless swirl of life. Chance be damned.

—

Today's orders: *Vanessa and Virginia* by Susan Sellers, *Facéties de chats* by Sébastien Perez and Benjamin Lacombe, *Gli estivi* by Luca Ricci, *Love at First Sight* by Wisława Szymborska, *At Fault* by Kate Chopin, *L'orto di un perdigiorno* by Pia Pera.

April 14, 2021

On the morning of April 14, 1930, the Russian poet Vladimir Mayakovsky left his house and returned shortly afterwards, extremely agitated. He was wearing a light yellow shirt he'd bought on Boulevard de la Madeleine, in Paris—a pale echo of the bright yellow blouse he'd wear for his performances. At 10:11 he shot himself through the heart.

At 10:00 a.m. on May 25, 2019, a man walked down the beautiful street that is Via Roma in Taormina, Sicily. He made for the usual café, where he ordered his usual coffee, then walked on in the direction of the sea, took out a gun, and shot himself.

That man was Sergio Claudio Perroni, translator, editor, author, lovable curmudgeon, perfectionist, Italian voice of Edward Carey. His death haunts me; not a day goes by that I don't think about it. I connect it to Mayakovsky's for a simple reason: theirs are both "active" suicides, provocative, choreographed almost, nothing short of performances.

> *And so they say—"the incident is closed"*
> *the love boat smashed up*
> *on the dreary routine.*
> *I'm through with life*
> *and [we] should absolve*
> *from mutual hurts,*
> *afflictions and spleen.*

This was Mayakovsky's suicide note.

Sergio, instead, told his wife, Cettina, as he got out of the shower that the book he was working on, *L'infinito di amare* (To Love) was progressing well. In her sweet voice, Cettina recalled their last moments together. That morning, Sergio made some coffee and put on "Can't Take My Eyes Off You" by Frankie Valli. At 8:00 a.m. he left and at 8:29 he called to say there was no need for her to leave the house, he'd be grabbing newspapers and cigarettes on his way back. That was the last time she heard his voice. They'd hugged at the door as if it were the first time, or the last, as they did *every* time.

I worked on many of his books, all of them exquisitely crafted, always swimming against the tide of contemporary trends. The first time I met him he was wearing (and I subsequently learned he only ever wore) Blundstone boots, about which he waxed lyrical. I immediately bought a pair and immediately understood that, as well as excellent taste in footwear, that man possessed an encyclopedic knowledge of the entire corpus of world literature, both classical and modern. His fierce tempers were legendary, but to me he was an uncompromising maverick, a true artist, one of the last of his kind. I liked him the way he was; I wouldn't have changed a single thing about him.

Then, inevitably, we had a disagreement, I can't even remember over what. But it didn't change my opinion of him—he may have been mad at me, but I was still on his side. When the editor of a literary supplement told me he'd heard Perroni didn't care for said supplement, I still sided with Perroni. We're all entitled to our opinions, authors all the more so—we're not sheep. What can I say? I went back to Lucignana, and Perroni planned his suicide.

His last books once again caught me by surprise—it is as though something inside him had softened. They're fables, tales, poetry, music, dreams. In *La bambina che somigliava alle cose scomparse* (The Girl Who Looked Like Lost Things) the protagonist, Pulce (Flea), runs away from home and from the things she's "supposed to be" and finds out she can turn into what people are looking for. She is their wish come true. *Entro a volte nel tuo sonno* (I Sometimes Visit Your Dreams) is yet another masterpiece. Reading it out loud makes me cry, so I have to read it quietly. I can feel Sergio hiding in that silence, with his Blundstones and his childlike smile.

Boris Pasternak wrote a poem about Mayakovsky's death (translated into English by Don Mager), and that's the first thing I thought about on May 25, 2019. Not about "passive" suicides—but a proud declaration, a leap into immortality:

You lunged over and over trying to crash
Into the ranks of youthful sagas.

—

Today's orders: *A Vindication of the Rights of Women* by Mary Wollstonecraft, *A Tree Grows in Brooklyn* by Betty Smith, *The House in Paris* by Elizabeth Bowen, *Leaving Home* by Anita Brookner.

April 16, 2021

We threw Mama a big party yesterday—there were pastries from De Servi, bubbly (sweet for her, dry for us), and presents. She was wearing a black silk dress with orange flowers and her pearls, and the mayor, as usual, turned up in his sash. She even made the local papers.

Lots of people came in small groups—my brother, Donatella and Graziano, Tiziana, Francesca, Marta. Mama chatted for half an hour to my cousin Luciana, who is the same age as me, thinking she was the Luciana who used to live next door when she was a little girl, and whom I imagine is long dead now. Mama seemed so happy to talk to her. I think she genuinely prefers the company of shadows—we, the living, are all a bit alien to her. We're so recent, too recent to be a part of her real life. Today she came up with the idea that the house we live in is not in fact a house, but a hospital we made up to look like a house to fool her. Had she known, she'd never have moved in.

Before he died, Uncle Fernando shouted, "Mama!" from his bedroom window for three months straight. He hadn't lost his mind—quite simply, like my mother, like all old people, he was looking for his home, which is always the home we grew up in. Childhood holds sway over all other seasons of life. It makes no difference whether it was happy or unhappy; that is where we will always return to answer for our actions. I think this is because childhood is completely devoid of ambition, of any interest in status, roles, or accolades—except for the need to love and be loved.

Today the government will issue new Covid restriction guidelines. I'm trying to stay positive, so I'll mow the lawn, paint the Frida Kahlo sun lounger, and order the little wrought-iron sofa which I'm planning to put under the plum tree. Someone ordered *Emily Dickinson's Herbarium* today, triggering the usual panic that I won't be able to get more copies.

—

Today's orders: *Emily Dickinson's Herbarium* by Emily Dickinson, *Manderley Forever: A Biography of Daphne du Maurier* by Tatiana de Rosnay, *Noi* by Paolo Di Stefano, *Quiet Chaos* by Sandro Veronesi, *Fever* by Jonathan Bazzi.

April 24, 2021

I spent several days in Florence with Laura, Mirto, and Peaches—a happy-go-lucky family with lots of non-rules and their own idiosyncratic habits, just like Pippi Longstocking's. As soon as I stepped outside, however, a cloud came over me: I hated walking under the sun on those impossibly flat streets. In Lucignana streets go either up or down—it keeps you on your toes, always, literally and metaphorically.

A few things happened while I was away. Mery—sweet, elegant Mery, who was born in Lucignana and then moved to Massa Carrara—passed away at the age of ninety-two. Redenta had already left us, and so the daily chorus that used to bind Florence, Massa, and Genoa together went quiet forever. My mother, Redenta, and Mery had clung to each other and bickered like little girls all these years. Lucignana always dominated their conversations: the latest gossip, how was such-and-such, who lived in the houses they hadn't lived in for years. We hadn't seen Mery in a long time, so we will always remember her tall, elegant, with a bouffant sixties hairdo. Her ashes arrived in Lucignana last Saturday. She's home.

Meanwhile Irma, our neighbor, fell off a ladder during one of her extreme weeding raids, and is now having to wear a chest brace for a month. Once, she cut off a vine that hung limply in an abandoned garden outside my window. I'd written a poem about that vine and the happiness it brought me every morning. When I saw Irma's savage pruning, I almost cried.

I've noticed Alberto Manguel often speaks of "moving" passages in novels—for instance when Frankenstein's monster enters the hermit's cabin and apologizes for intruding. To be moved by something is to experience an altered psychological state—calm waters suddenly ruffled by the wind. In the case of a "strong" reader such as Manguel, it's especially interesting to observe what, exactly, triggers this particular emotion—especially if it's triggered by what Orwell would dub a "good bad book," which is to say, a book with no literary pretensions, but which continues to fascinate readers. I think this has something to do with comfort reading: you read to be comforted, and cry when the comfort kicks in. "Comfort" has long been anathema in the Italian literary scene, dominated for decades by avant-garde and structuralist cliques. Nowadays, thank goodness, we read Annie Ernaux, Joan Didion, and Jamaica Kincaid.

Martin Latham, who runs Waterstones Canterbury, recently published a book—incidentally, he also abandoned a brilliant career at the University of Hertfordshire to sell books. The first chapter of *The Bookseller's Tale* is dedicated to comfort reads, the ones we come across, not the ones we choose—like love—the ones that assuage our fears, the ones we keep close to our hearts like a secret and never mention in public, because they are and always will be a private matter. If I were to meet Martin, say in a café in Canterbury, and if he asked about my comfort reads, this would be my answer:

- *Mignon* by Berthe Franel
- *Little Dorrit* by Charles Dickens
- *Pecos Bill* by Eric Blair
- *Pippi Longstocking* by Astrid Lindgren

Latham argues that these are the books that strongly influence what we'd like to be when we grow up, or indeed anticipate what we will be. Based on this, my secret reads point to some sort of split personality—on one end, an unhappy little girl who looks after society's outcasts, on the other, a dynamic, happy-go-lucky child perfectly capable of fending for herself. How many times have I read the story of Pecos Bill, who, as an infant, falls from his parents' cart and finds himself alone in the Texas desert, surrounded by cactus and coyotes? The coyotes end up raising him as one of their own, and it's not until he is found again that he realizes he is, in fact, human. Bill can use his snake, Shake, as a lasso or a whip, which I'm sure did wonders for my mental health (and my fear of that snake that lurked in the fields of Lucignana, looking for young girls' throats to slither into).

—

Today's orders: *Little* by Edward Carey, *La virtù dell'orto* by Pia Pera, *An Unnecessary Woman* by Rabih Alameddine, *Farewell, Ghosts* by Nadia Terranova, *View with a Grain of Sand* by Wisława Szymborska,

Consolations of the Forest: Alone in a Cabin on the Siberian Taiga by Sylvain Tesson, *Les Lendemains* by Mélissa Da Costa.

April 26, 2021

Today we fully reopen to the wider public for the first time after months of "red" and "amber" tier restrictions. Sadly, the weather's not looking great. We've let our followers know we'll be open on Saturday and Sunday by reservation only, max fifteen people per hour. Let's see what happens.

Last weekend we had our first visitors from outside the council area, a couple from Florence. The sun was shining; they'd had enough of being cooped up, and decided to set off. I always enjoy seeing readers in the flesh, each on their own reading journey, all seemingly happy to be here. On Sunday the family of readers from Filicaia came back—Mama, Dad, Elia (nine) and Matilde (twelve). Once again they were debating "which book to get Mama—Elia was pushing for *All Passion Spent* by Vita Sackville-West, Matilde for *Vera* by Elizabeth von Arnim. In the end the father talked everyone around to *A Tree Grows in Brooklyn* by Betty Smith, while the mother herself, having enjoyed Nadia Terranova's *Gli anni al contrario* (The Years in Reverse) picked up her latest novel, *Farewell, Ghosts*.

In less than two weeks Tina's book will be out, the one she wrote during the first three months of lockdown. The excellent title— *Sinfonia domestica* (Domestic Symphony)—unfolds as a chorus of voices and thoughts from a family of four (plus dog) forced to spend every minute of every day together in Milan. The beauty of the book is that this family appears to slowly take shape day after day before our eyes, as if it had sprung up out of nothing during the pandemic. Tina, too, has the gift of irony, which I lack.

Meanwhile, another batch of Anna's jams has arrived—Virginia Woolf's (bitter oranges and peaty whisky) and Charlotte Brontë's (mandarin and vanilla). Natalie finally replied to confirm my order, and Julie wrote to say Mike got in touch to arrange for our tea to be picked up, seeing as he'll be coming to Italy on May 20. Everything finally seems to be falling into place.

I'm reviewing our catalogue, which is the most exciting part of my job. Yesterday Donatella and I finally got around to painting the Frida Kahlo sun lounger, now a lovely sage green, and even repainted the bookshop floor in a new shade of bluish gray. Graziano cut the grass, which in just one week had grown an awful lot. We kept looking back as we left, as proud of that place as of a daughter on her first day of school.

—

Today's orders: *Les Lendemains* by Mélissa Da Costa, *Cortile nostalgia* by Giuseppina Torregrossa, *Il giardino che vorrei* by Pia Pera, *History of the Rain* by Niall Williams.

April 27, 2021

I'd never have remembered Pecos Bill if it weren't for Latham's book. A lost child who invented a life for himself among the creatures that took him in: coyotes and snakes. A nobody who'd become an amazing cowboy because of all the things he'd learned, as a child, from animals and cacti. His will always be a different language, one forged outside human conventions and in close contact with nature.

Pecos, Pippi, and Pinocchio—yes, *Pinocchio* was another one of my most treasured books as a child, specifically the 1963 edition with a preface by Dino Buzzati, originally a special edition exclusively for the children of Italian doctors. It was a huge book, as tall as a four-year-old, wonderfully illustrated by Alberto Longoni, who managed to confer real depth and humanity to a character usually depicted as frivolous and uncaring. It just so happened that at the time, Auntie Feny worked as a governess for a famous cardiologist in Lucca. Viviana, his wife, adored my aunt, and she knew Fenysia had a niece who loved books. And so it was that this little gem made its way to me, completing the trio of "adventurous Ps" who just about saved my life.

Because my life definitely needed saving—my brother had married and we'd moved to the house with no bathroom. I don't know if this is a dream or an actual memory, but to this day I can still picture my brother's wedding. After the ceremony and the reception, the bride and groom were saying their goodbyes before heading off to their honeymoon in Capri. The guests had gathered on the main square to wish them well—the bride was sitting in the car, engine already running, while the groom, one leg in the car, wrestled with a desperate little girl who refused to let go of his other leg, sobbing uncontrollably in front of the whole town. The love she'd kept hidden for six years was now on display for everyone to see.

That night, the little girl began to suffer from a perception disorder. People's voices would suddenly drop into nothingness, things would get smaller and smaller until they disappeared from sight, her tongue would grow into a huge foreign body inside her mouth, and if she touched an object it would feel enormous, as if it were about to crush her hand. Sight, hearing, touch, taste, were all compromised: nothing but shadows. She could still smell the hell she lived in, though. Not knowing what to do about those strange symptoms, her mother would take her to the ophthalmologist's—needless to say, there was nothing wrong with her eyes. But she still complained that she "saw things far away." There was only one doctor who could cure her, and it was her father. Everything would go back to normal if he sat on her bed and asked: "You see things far away, you say? So you can see Auntie Feny in Genoa?"

Irony saves lives. But not everyone has that gift—Pascoli probably didn't either, although he was an exquisite poet. And he also knew a thing or two about faraway things. This is from "Nebbia" ("Fog," translated into English by Geoffrey Brock), one of his masterpieces:

> Hide what is far from my eyes,
> pale fog, impalpable grey
> vapor climbing the light
> of the coming day,
> after the storm-streaked night,
> the rockfall skies . . .

So many books have been written about faraway things, about a shrinking world that disappears from sight, about loss, rockfalls, abandonment—pages upon pages of angry tears and sorrows. Pecos loses his parents, Pippi gazes dreamily at a candle, imagining the return of her father, Pinocchio must face the most unsettling of changes—and yet . . . Reading was the cure, the magic that gave me my senses back: faraway things were once more within reach; I could hear the rockfalls in the skies. Now I can see, hear, touch, and taste without fear of disappearing into nothingness.

It is 7:00 a.m.; the rain has stopped; I'm reviewing our catalogue, my Emerenc will be here shortly.

—

Today's orders: *The Other Woman* by Colette, *Due vite* by Emanuele Trevi, *The Bookshop* by Penelope Fitzgerald, *Il bosco del confine* by Federica Manzon, *Il giardino che vorrei* by Pia Pera, *Loving Frank* by Nancy Horan, *Storia di Luis Sepúlveda e del suo gatto Zorba* by Ilide Carmignani.

April 29, 2021

"Where are you off to?" asked my brother yesterday, when he came to see Mama.

"To look at the garden," I answered. He must think I'm odd—to him, woods and fields are not there to look at, but to make use of. He worked at the steelworks in Fornaci di Barga all his life, but when he turned sixty he retired and started living his life the way he likes it—that is, in his log cabin in Fontanaccio, or up and down the fields in his tractor, or, better still, spoiling his grandchildren. All his grandchildren adore him; they always have, same as I adored him. I don't think we ever had a Christmas dinner where Fabio and David didn't sit either side of him. He's seventy-eight now and impossibly handsome. He set the bar for every single man I have loved—if they didn't fit that particular mold, they were out. When his daughter Vania was born, I was so jealous that if we were left alone I would pinch her hard until she cried. She was just a baby, but I was a seven-year-old who saw things far away—I wasn't exactly having an easy time of it either.

Giulia told me we have twenty people booked in for next weekend, and quite a few reservations for May and June already. This makes me happy. I can't wait to meet our book lovers again, find out what they're reading, what they'll buy.

The cottage is ready: the floorboards have been painted, as have the sun loungers; the roses are blossoming; the peonies are taking their time, quietly going about their business. Then there's the hill beyond the fence, blanketed in a rainbow of wild flowers: white, yellow, purple, red. Seeing as I talk to them every morning, I thought it only polite to learn their names: cardoon, columbine, dandelion, buttercup, wild carrot, fleabane, sorrel, speedwell—plus two lonely poppies who just couldn't wait until July. Our plum tree is magnificent. The trunk itself is just beyond the fence, but the branches weigh heavy over the garden, a cozy cocoon of dark-red leaves. I'm debating what to put underneath, maybe a little iron table and chairs with a candle, maybe the two Adirondacks, but anything would look good there, really.

It's 7:30 a.m.; I'll be out shortly doing the rounds in the garden, checking on flowers and grass—a ritual I've been performing every morning since I came back here. Nothing is overlooked, not a single stem, twig, petal.

Our twelve-square-meter cottage has a little window that looks out on Monte Prato Fiorito. In pride of place on the windowsill you will always find one of these three books on a little iron stand: *Virginia Woolf's Garden* by Caroline Zoob, *Emily Dickinson's Herbarium*, and *Alice's Adventures in Wonderland* illustrated by Tenniel. It's really quite a window, endlessly photographed by whoever sets foot in the cottage. Aside from these, other permanent fixtures include anything by Pia Pera, *The Green Wiccan Herbal* by Silja, and a long list of books about nature as an instrument of redemption.

- *Les Lendemains* by Mélissa Da Costa
- *Elizabeth and Her German Garden* by Elizabeth von Arnim
- *Pour un herbier* by Colette
- *La Botanique* by Jean-Jacques Rousseau
- *The Way Through the Woods* by Long Litt Woon
- *Trees* by Hermann Hesse
- *My Wild Garden* by Meir Shalev
- *Wild Fruits* by Henry David Thoreau

- *Der englische Botaniker* by Nicole C. Vosseler
- *"Cherry" Ingram: The Englishman Who Saved Japan's Blossoms* by Naoko Abe
- *The Metamorphosis of Plants* by J. W. von Goethe
- *The Gardener's Year* by Karel Čapek
- *Can Anything Stop Slugs?: A Gardener's Collection of Pesky Problems and Surprising Solutions* by Guy Barter
- *From Tiny Seeds* by Émilie Vast
- *In giardino non si è mai soli* by Paolo Pejrone
- *Sprechende Blumen* by Isabel Kranz
- *Think like a Mountain* by Aldo Leopold
- *The Illustrated Garden Book* by Vita Sackville-West
- *How Forests Think* by Eduardo Kohn

—

Today's orders: *Mes maisons d'écrivains* by Évelyne Bloch-Dano, *Amulet* by Roberto Bolaño, *This Wild Darkness: The Story of My Death* by Harold Brodkey, *Leaving Home* by Anita Brookner.

May

"I'll take this one," said a ten-year-old girl handing me Michela Murgia's latest feminist essay.

"Is this for you? I'm not sure you'll enjoy it . . ." I ventured, assuming she was tricked by the approachable cover.

She looked me straight in the eye: "I'll be just fine."

And that's just the way Iris is. Her elder sister, more introverted or simply not as forward, is called Ester, like Esther in Katja Petrowskaja's *Maybe Esther*, like Magda Szabó's Eszter in *The Fawn*. She's only fourteen, but she picked Katharina von Arx's travel memoir and Martin Latham's *The Bookseller's Tale*. They bought *Spring* by Ali Smith for their mother, while the father opted for Elizabeth Brundage's thriller *All Things Cease to Appear*—he's a builder, not a regular reader, and needed something to keep him glued to the page. They came from Montopoli in the Valdarno region in their camper, which hadn't been used in months. Truth be told, Ester had already come with some friends, and ended up dragging her whole family to Lucignana. This, too, is Italy—not just cathedrals and frescoes and picturesque towns, but people, real people, families that defy the brute statistics that frame so much of our discourse.

Another group stood out too—young visitors from Florence who had clearly done their homework. They wandered around the garden taking hundreds of photos, commenting: "My mother would love this," "Just a couple of snaps for Mama," "My mother's coming tomorrow with her friends."

From which I conclude (in case anyone had any doubt) that the publishing industry is almost entirely propped up by women, and these mothers in particular were able to pass on their love of books to their children. Who'd have thought that, in this day and age, a group of twenty-somethings' first reaction upon seeing something beautiful would be to share it with their mothers?

A bookshop is a school—a window looking out on a world that we only think we know. But to really understand the world we have to read, because those who write are always inspired by something that doesn't quite fit the mold. And when things don't add up, authors must face the paradox of life and venture into the darkness of the human mind—become at one with that darkness, even—there is no other way. Elsa Morante knew this when, in her seminal novel *History*, she described how a young, desperate German soldier, Gunther, raped the schoolteacher Ida in Rome. She delves deep into Gunther's desperation, into that "horrendous, desolate melancholy," and finds Ida reflected in it, sees how their childhoods still cling to them both like a physical impairment. She finds what they share, as well as what makes them different. We have to get used to this kind of author perspective, to seeing things from behind, from below, from above, close up, and far away. We'll lose all our reference points, our rules, but we might just understand something of that darkness. Evil is unknown always, and we're forever scrambling to comprehend how it comes to be.

—

Today's orders: *The Deep Blue Between* by Ayesha Harruna Attah, *Il libro della gioia perpetua* by Emanuele Trevi, *Sweet Sorrow* by David Nicholls, *Nomadland* by Jessica Bruder, *Giallo d'Avola* by Paolo Di Stefano, *Vita meravigliosa* by Patrizia Cavalli.

May 14, 2021

"Mama, I want to be little again and just be with you all the time."
That's what she said. She was crying. There's nothing for it—when
your daughter says these words to you, you just drop everything and
go to her. I made her meatballs in marinara sauce, chicken soup,
mashed potatoes——I re-created our little family bubble. She was
only afraid of failing her exams, of growing up too, perhaps. Then I
came back, and thank goodness Alessandra could cover for me. Every
time I leave, I find my mother's aged three years in one week—she
can never be alone; she'll fall and demand to be "taken home."

We don't have to understand everything in life, but we do need
to find compassion and let it in, deep inside our bones, let it guide
our thoughts and our actions. That's how we pick up someone else's
thread, and slowly pull them out—and then another thread, and
another, and another again. We shouldn't stop to look back at the
people we've saved; that's bad luck—we must always look forward,
to the next thread.

If I looked back right now, I'd see Natalie's parcel—44 euros in
shipping fees alone, and that's on top of the 129 euros I had to fork
out for customs duties. There goes my margin. What an ugly thing
bureaucracy is—I imagine there must be someone whose job consists
entirely of manufacturing these obstacles, a permanent secretary
perhaps, in the Ministry for the Allocation of Obstacles. Alessandra
would tell them to go fuck themselves.

Luckily, Lucignana's lively expat community includes Nati and
Nira Sharona, who are from Tel Aviv, and maybe we'll manage to
have them bring us some stockings in the future—we're discussing
it. So we'd have Mike for our teas, and Nati and Nira for the literary
stockings. Then there's Prudence who always brings us cupcakes,

William who plays the piano, and Virginia who looks just like her namesake.

—

Today's orders: *La nave per Kobe* by Dacia Maraini, *Memorie di una contadina* by Lev Tolstoy and T. A. Kuzminskaja, *Apprendista di felicità* by Pia Pera, *The Penelopiad* by Margaret Atwood, *Little* by Edward Carey, *The Adversary: A True Story of Monstrous Deception* by Emmanuel Carrère, *Sinfonia domestica* by Tina Guiducci.

May 16, 2021

There was a slight drizzle yesterday, so we moved the two tables under the pergola to welcome the visitors who, despite the weather, had come from Florence, Bologna, Reggio Emilia. Since restrictions were lifted, every day brings something unexpected. Curious tales flow in from the sage-green gate and catch us unawares—the stuff of cult novels, fairy tales, art-house films.

Yesterday two anglers appeared under the rain. One tall, heavy, with a friendly smile and kind eyes, the other wiry, springy. They looked straight out of Robert Altman's *Short Cuts*, a film based on Raymond Carver's short stories. I thought I wouldn't have anything for them, and I was wrong. The one with the kind eyes told me he'd read all my poems, and that they reminded him somewhat of his favorite poet, Robert Frost.

Jesus.

That'd be the Robert Frost who said that "a poem begins with a lump in the throat; a homesickness or a love sickness." *His friend, though*—I kept thinking, wrongly—*I won't have anything for his friend.* "When Lawrence Ferlinghetti died," said friend began, "and

I reviewed my Beat collection, I realized I didn't have anything by Gregory Corso." After praising the clear waters of the streams near Lucignana—Surricchiana, Dezza, Segone—the two angler friends left with *The Wild Iris* by Louise Glück and *A Coney Island of the Mind* by Lawrence Ferlinghetti. I thought of the great critic Harold Bloom, sitting in Nantucket next to his friend, who fished while Bloom read Whitman out loud ("when I desperately need to assuage grief," wrote Bloom in *The Western Canon*, "there is a particular appropriateness in chanting Whitman"):

> *In the dooryard fronting an old farm-house near the white-*
> *   wash'd palings,*
> *Stands the lilac-bush tall-growing with heart-shaped leaves*
> *   of rich green,*
> *With many a pointed blossom rising delicate, with the*
> *   perfume strong I love,*
> *With every leaf a miracle—and from this bush in the*
> *   dooryard,*
> *With delicate-color'd blossoms and heart-shaped leaves of*
> *   rich green,*
> *A sprig with its flower I break.*

That's how I imagine our angler friends, wading up rock pools, trekking across the woods while reciting a poem by Glück or Ferlinghetti. Needless to say, whatever they catch is immediately released back into the stream. Fishing is just therapy.

—

Today's order is really quite special—a wedding gift.

For the bride: *Tōkyō tutto l'anno* by Laura Imai Messina, *A People's History of Heaven* by Mathangi Subramanian, *Mujeres que compran flores* by Vanessa Montfort, *What You Can See from Here* by Mariana Leky.

For the groom: *La Fille de Debussy* by Damien Luce, *L'incredibile cena dei fisici quantistici* by Gabriella Greison, *Wasan: Sangaku mondai no kyozaika: yasui konpiragu hono sangaku sandai shikiei kara* by Toshimitsu Hirano, *Il dimenticatoio: Dizionario delle parole perdute* by various authors.

For both: bookmarks, notebooks, tea.

May 17, 2021

Yesterday Donatella and I spent the afternoon repotting flowers under a brooding sky, which didn't fail to deliver the storms it had been threatening all day.

I love the ever-changing landscape of storms, where the light appears to move in sync with the wind itself, shaping new horizons. It reminds me of Alberto Giacometti and Samuel Beckett endlessly readjusting the little skeletal tree the sculptor had created for the restaging of *Waiting for Godot* at the Odéon, in Paris—the only décor on the minimalist stage. Giacometti would move a branch an inch to the left and step aside to check if it worked: *oui, peut-être*. Then Beckett would do the same, lower a branch, step back to check. *Oui, peut-être*. Just like the two fastidious artists, the wind reshuffles clouds and leaves while light follows closely behind, painting ridges, plains, paths, and clearings where there were none. Even Monte Prato Fiorito had vanished at one point, as if it had never been there before. It's back now, basking in the morning sun.

"In the purest of countries, the country you can breathe, the real country," wrote Simone Weil to Joë Bousquet—well, I can see the "real country" from my bookshop, so different from the fake landscapes that seem so prevalent everywhere. Everywhere except from here.

Meanwhile, a personal tragedy of mine has been playing out in the background. My mother can barely walk, she keeps falling and is no longer able to go up or down the stairs that lead to her room, so I put in an application for a place at the nursing home in Coreglia. Samantha, whose mother, Roberta, is from Lucignana, works there—she is joy personified and extremely reliable. That said, it's a difficult choice, and I am racked with guilt. Am I doing the right thing? Am I abandoning her? While I torture myself with these questions, Mama and Ernesto sit on the sofa, hugging, holding hands—she's dozing; he's crying.

I'll go down to the garden to check on the flowers we repotted yesterday, see if we put them in the right spot. I'll take some photos and send them to Donatella—I'll be the Giacometti to her Beckett.

—

Today's orders: *L'architettrice* by Melania G. Mazzucco, *The Penelopiad* by Margaret Atwood, *The Women's War* by Alexandre Dumas, *La felicità degli altri* by Carmen Pellegrino, *Winterbienen* by Norbert Scheuer, *Diario di bordo di uno scrittore* by Björn Larsson, *Storielle al contrario* by Vivian Lamarque.

May 20, 2021

My bookshop is like a personal heaven to me—and you wouldn't lock up the gates of heaven. When I arrived in Florence back in 1979, I'd only just got my driving license and drove around in my father's blue minivan—everyone wondered why I never locked it. My father never locked a car in his life; my mother locks the main door by 5:00 p.m.

every day—two different approaches to life. Someone might break in, steal, damage, wreck my possessions—that may well be. But I want no part in it. My father and I, we belong in the "real country" where things are wrecked, where people cry and rage. My father and I decided we wouldn't live in a world of locked doors.

Fabiola came to the bookshop on Sunday morning and I gave her a copy of *Her Mother's Face*, a children's book by Roddy Doyle. It's the story of a little girl who lost her mother and, after a series of mysterious encounters, finds her again as a grown woman, reflected in her mirror. Fabiola stood there crying in the middle of the bookshop.

My father refusing to lock his car, Maicol wondering where the wind has gone, Fabiola crying over Roddy Doyle's book, Ernesto and Mama hugging on the sofa, the anglers reading Glück and Ferlinghetti—these are all fragments of that "breathable country" Simone Weil spoke of. These are fragments of my new life here in Lucignana.

—

Today's orders: *A Good Man Is Hard to Find and Other Stories* by Flannery O'Connor, *A Frozen Woman* by Annie Ernaux, *L'isola riflessa* by Fabrizia Ramondino, *Isolario italiano* by Fabio Fiori, *Pariser Rechenschaft* by Thomas Mann.

May 24, 2021

Mama's gone and done it. She got up despite being told not to, climbed two steps, and fell on her back. We'd begged her to wait in bed just one more minute, long enough to turn off the stove. One minute. Sure enough, she did the exact opposite. The day before she'd told us all to get lost—she wanted to get up and "go home" to her sisters, from which I conclude she has started talking to shadows for good. Weddings, children, divorces—it's all been wiped out. Now there's only her childhood home, eating polenta for breakfast, lunch, and dinner, little Polda and Fenysia waiting for her to go dancing in Tereglio. You can't blame her, really—if I'd grown up with that combination of poverty and love, I too would want to "go home." I'd be right on Auntie Polda's knees, singing, "Horsey horsey, don't you stop, / Just let your feet go clippetty-clop, / The tail goes swish and the wheels go 'round, / Giddy up, we're homeward bound."

Mama, instead, is now in hospital in Castelnuovo, Garfagnana, with a broken cervical vertebra and wrist, plus a few cracked ribs and a bruised lung to boot. That said, Dr. Banti maintains she is calm and content. We had a bit of a choppy start, Dr. Banti and I, but then we spoke on the phone and immediately got on, as it so often happens between women. Next time I go visit Mama I'll bring the doctor a copy of *Memoirs of a Woman Doctor* by Nawal El Saadawi; I'm sure she'll enjoy it.

Whenever an ambulance arrives in Lucignana the news spreads like wildfire, as if the houses themselves were relaying the message. I'm convinced Jan Koum, who created WhatsApp, must have studied how communication works in little mountain villages: as soon as someone changes their status, anyone connected to that person will know. We're the original social network, a network forged through First Communions, confirmations, imaginary footballer boyfriends, the first taste of those forbidden pleasures, and pretending to be famous bands. Speaking of which, I'd forgotten to mention the Kessler twins, two long-legged, leotard-clad German showgirls on Italy's most popular Saturday night show, *Canzonissima*. Luisa and I would practice their choreography for weeks, then reenact it at school (including a rather daring jump from the windowsills in the main corridor).

It's raining again—we might as well be in November. But that didn't stop visitors coming from Bologna, Verona, and Modena, as well as from all over Tuscany, as always. A couple carried a pile of books to one of the tables, discussed them, and ended up buying half—it was amazing to listen to their conversation. Another girl brought us flowers—she'd driven all the way from Verona and braved the Radici Pass to get to us, a true hero.

By the way, my daughter's WhatsApp status reads: "My dream is steady jobs for all my friends." She won't be locking her car either; I feel it in my bones. She once walked four kilometers from the Lucca train station to visit her granddad in the hospital—he still cries when he thinks about it. As does she. My mother's status is much more straightforward: "I live with my sister," she announced to the nurses. There's no clawing her back from the past now.

—

Today's orders: *Hotel Bella Vista* by Colette, *La hija única* by Guadalupe Nettel, *La più amata* by Teresa Ciabatti, *Mujeres que compran flores* by Vanessa Montfort, *I malcontenti* by Paolo Nori, *Addio mio Novecento* by Aldo Nove.

May 25, 2021

Raffaella has just put in an order: *Les Lendemains* by Mélissa Da Costa, *An Unnecessary Woman* by Rabih Alameddine, *The Rose Garden* and *The Springs of Affection* by Maeve Brennan, *Vera* by Elizabeth von Arnim, *The German House* by Annette Hess, *Somewhere Towards the End* by Diana Athill, *History of the Rain* by Niall Williams, and *A Pure Clear Light* by Madeleine St John. She left me another voice message saying she already knows what she'll order next—I do love her voice messages and her French *r*'s. She's truly invaluable, often flagging bugs on our website, or shipping issues—a bit like having an agent in Milan.

I would love for Isabella, Tina, and Raffaella to meet and form some sort of Lucignana enclave up north—I can see them already, chatting over Prosecco in a chic café on Corso Genova. They're all from Milan, read the same books, live in similar houses, and among them have six children of the same age—what exactly are they waiting for? Off to an aperitivo on the canal, I say. I'll have to invite them all here as soon as iced tea and Prosecco season starts, which is when temperatures sit comfortably over 28°C. I like bringing people together who belong together; I have a sixth sense for these things.

Today I went to visit Mama in the hospital—five minutes is all I was allowed. My brother came along too. The two of us behaving like normal siblings is quite unprecedented—we drove there together like brother and sister; I got out like a normal sister would; he parked like a normal brother would. It took me fifty-five years to bring us together again, and forty-eight to get Mama and Dad on speaking terms again.

I'm nothing if not patient, working away in my little corner, always looking like I'm busy doing something else. Sometimes it takes a lifetime to heal a wound; other times you just have to forget about it, think of something else, cry over something else. It's just another job, really, or perhaps more of a vocation: I'm a bookseller who specializes in fixing things.

Today, finally, we'll have some sun. It's 6:00 a.m., and I must go to check on my peonies, my roses, and all the other flowers we repotted.

—

Today's orders: *Quando anche le donne si misero a dipingere* by Anna Banti, *Quatre Peintres* by Marcel Proust, *The House in Paris* by

Elizabeth Bowen, *Second Nature* by Michael Pollan, *Verdeggiando: Male erbe e altre delizie* by Pia Pera, *The Secret Lives of Trees* by Peter Wohlleben.

May 27, 2021

On May 27, 1931, Rolando was born, the first of Tullio and Orlandina's children, three boys and three girls. Life netted him an ex-wife (my mother), a daughter (me), and a great love for which he abandoned both. The "other woman," Eli, six years his senior, sharp and sweet, had in turn abandoned her husband and children to spend her life surrounded by cows and rabbits—a passion she shared with my father, with whom she was madly in love. She died of cancer ten years ago. Cows aside, she was always extremely elegant, with a coquettish streak—pink lace, fuchsia coats.

For a year after her death my father would go to cry over her grave every day. He cried all the time, including the day when his neighbor, Agnese, saw him in tears in the garden and stopped to console him. She stroked his cheek—bless her, she was eighty; there was no harm in it. A few days later they'd moved in together. Dad called to say he'd found a new girlfriend. For a year now Agnese has been suffering from a particularly violent form of Alzheimer's and had to move in with her daughter so she could contain her sudden bouts of rage. Rolando visits her every day; they talk about the good old days when they were children, and all the things they did together (when, in fact, they hadn't even met).

I'll surprise him today. Alessandra and I will get him a cake from De Servi and sing "Happy Birthday." Mama, meanwhile, sleeps in her hospital bed, sedated.

Life's just chaos sometimes. Florence feels so far away with its glittery elites and desperation on its streets. I'm here, looking at Monte Prato Fiorito, which I photographed again yesterday at dawn. As the sun rose, it revealed an orange-pink aura glittering around the twin domes—I saw it. I have proof.

There's a book that sells really well, *Hokusai: Thirty-Six Views of Mount Fuji* by Amélie Balcou. It's a collection of Katsushika Hokusai's landscape prints of the Japanese sacred mountain from different viewpoints and in different seasons, which were originally published in the late nineteenth century. You don't need to travel the world to see the world; you can just sit still in one place and let nature display the infinite facets of her beauty. If we count all my childhood drawings, and the various analogue and digital photos, I'm positive I have way more than thirty-six views of Monte Prato Fiorito. We fall in love, break up, cry, and the twin domes are there, as they have always been, ever-changing and immutable. I simply cannot be away from them. Here I am, looking at *my* mountain, ecstatic. Truly ecstatic. Happy birthday, Dad.

—

Today's orders: *My Wild Garden* by Meir Shalev, *Sinfonia domestica* by Tina Guiducci, *Vies conjugales* by Bernard Quiriny, *La non mamma* by Susanna Tartaro, *Ribes e rose* by Enrica Borghi and Cristina Amodeo.

May 28, 2021

It's so frustrating to come across a promising book that didn't live up to its potential. I was captivated by *Legendäre Katzen und ihre*

Menschen (Legendary Cats and Their Humans) by Heike Reinecke and Andreas Schlieper, both by the topic and by the cover of the Italian edition—Frida Kahlo with a cat on her shoulder on a bright green background. I was expecting Marguerite Yourcenar, Wisława Szymborska—nothing. I skimmed through the book, dismayed: Hemingway, Derrida, Chandler, Murakami, Baudelaire, Churchill. Thirty-two chapters in total, of which only five were dedicated to female humans. Famous male cat lovers beat famous female cat lovers 27–5—except the ref was looking the other way the whole time. I'm going to return all the copies I'd ordered.

We think we've won this particular battle; we haven't. Two years ago, Pierpaolo and I asked two esteemed professors to prepare ten university lectures dedicated to the most influential figures in twentieth-century Italian fiction and twentieth-century philosophy. Not a single one of the lectures they proposed focused on a woman. No Hannah Arendt or Simone Weil, no Maria Zambrano, Elsa Morante, Natalia Ginzburg, Anna Maria Ortese. Most worrying of all, the two esteemed professors were self-avowed liberals. The problem is that they simply defaulted to male authors; unless deliberately prodded in that direction, their brains on autopilot would not detect women. They have to really *think* about it.

I'm reading an extremely informative book by Rebecca Solnit, *Recollections of My Nonexistence*. In Solnit's "nonexistence" I see the many attempts to erase female voices that we experience from birth, and that so often fly under the radar of "invisible" referees (as outlandish as that may sound in this day and age). The invisible referees hide in our family, among our friends, in the films we love, in the songs we listen to, in the cartoons we watched as children.

That is why we must never tire of bringing the fight to them again and again. We may begin by rereading the first line of "Cat in an Empty Apartment," the most beautiful poem ever written about cats, by the Nobel laureate Wisława Szymborska, who happened to be born on the same day as me, July 2:

Die—you can't do that to a cat.

—

Today's orders: *Eating Animals* by Jonathan Safran Foer, *Girl, Woman, Other* by Bernardine Evaristo, *The Maids* by Junichiro Tanizaki, *L'unica persona nera nella stanza* by Nadeesha Uyangoda, *Difficoltà per le ragazze* by Rossana Campo, *Amy and Isabelle* by Elizabeth Strout, *Gli autunnali* by Luca Ricci.

May 29, 2021

Pia Pera didn't much care for roses—too pretentious, too perfect. My dear Pia, I will always be a devoted disciple of yours, but on this I cannot follow you. I am utterly fascinated by the beauty of the roses that are blossoming in my garden, and the peonies too. It is exhilarating to think that they are thriving because of me—my care, my devotion.

In his book *My Wild Garden*, the Israeli author Meir Shalev tells of how he crouches down on his hands and knees to prune, dig, and weed his garden, which at some point became his main reason for living. When the grass dries out and dies, Shalev is not bothered: he knows that his garden embodies the great stories of death and resurrection of ancient people who lived here—Phoenicians, Sumerians, Egyptians, Greeks. Stories based on the love and respect for nature which were the foundations of ancient cultures. When I'm in my garden, I won't answer my phone: I'm fully disconnected—I breathe.

I've started *Yoga* by Emmanuel Carrère. He tells us about his depression, about being committed to a psychiatric hospital, undergoing electroshock. Perhaps if he'd tried pruning a rosebush or keeping pests away from a grapevine it wouldn't have got to that point. It might have helped. A friend of mine, the poet Stefano Dal Bianco, once told me that there are only two things that will truly save your life: a happy childhood with a close-knit family, or being from hardworking farmer stock. He had the first; I, the second.

Today Alessandra (daughter of a sheep farmer) hugged me. Not something you'd expect from your average street-stomping, chain-smoking neighborhood thug. She opened her arms and I felt a tremendous heat radiating from her. I saw her family—her handsome husband, Claudio, her two boys, both so grown now—and I thought of how much warmth she must give them, in between all the "fuck offs" and "enough of your crap." Like an ever-burning stove.

—

Today's orders: *Mrs. Dalloway* by Virginia Woolf, *Yoga* by Emmanuel Carrère, *Alone* by August Strindberg, *The Misfits* by Arthur Miller, *Will o' the Mill* by Robert Louis Stevenson, *Come prima delle madri* by Simona Vinci.

May 31, 2021

In Sofia Segovia's *The Murmur of Bees*, Nana Reja, an old woman whose exact age is unknown (including to her), has been sitting on a rocking chair for thirty years, in the exact same spot. For winters, springs, summers, and autumns on end she just looks at the dirt road outside her house, at the sugarcane fields, at the mountains that hem in the valley; to her, this is like an exciting adventure, which surprises her every day with new colors, shadows, smells.

Nana Reja's town feels a lot like Gabriel García Márquez's Macondo, and a lot like Lucignana, too. I step on my balcony and Monte Prato Fiorito comes forward to greet me with its symphony of valleys, surprising me every evening, every morning, as it did the very first time I saw it.

Yesterday Fabiola came by and told me that her grandmother Egre, the great matriarch, in the last days of her life would often jump out of bed calling out to her dead sisters. Fabiola argues it can't be a coincidence—after all, what do we know of the Great Beyond? Is it so hard to believe that Egre's sisters would go to her, like Auntie Polda and Auntie Feny are doing right now with Mama?

This weekend the shop was a hive of activity—seventy people in total across Saturday and Sunday, good titles sold to deserving readers. Books need to get off the shelves every now and again and live a little, so I'd set aside two crates marked "great books" and "seriously great books" (and who's going to argue with that?) which people seemed to gravitate around—although our visitors always scan every corner of every shelf, regardless. Many came from Modena, a bizarre coincidence. On a map, it looks just on the other side of the Apennines from us, but it's nearly 150 kilometers of mountain roads. Be that as it may, there's no denying our bookshop can count on a community of devoted followers from Modena. I heard a girl say: "These steps! I've been dreaming of these steps!"

I'm exhausted, but happy. Lately I've been inviting some of the younger girls in the village to do some shifts at the bookshop, and so far Sandy and Rebecca have signed up. Another experiment of mine—I'm always looking for ways to open up more, be more inclusive, bring more people together. There's a lady from Rome who owns a house in Lucignana, and who refuses to say hello to me. For no particular reason, she decided to join the 30 percent of naysayers—God knows what she was told, that I eat children for breakfast maybe, whereas I spend hours contemplating Monte Prato Fiorito, which is my Fuji, my Ararat, my Kailash. Noah didn't build his Ark there and Shiva didn't make it his home, but many a witch danced on those rounded domes, leaving them pure, sublime, white as the *Narcissus poeticus* that covers them in spring. Will someone please tell the lady from Rome that I'm *poeticus* too and I've got swallows fluttering over my head, darting in and out of my windows?

—

Today's orders: *Sweet Sorrow* by David Nicholls, *Nomadland* by Jessica Bruder, *Himself* by Jess Kidd, *Les Lendemains* by Mélissa Da Costa, *The Winter of Our Discontent* by John Steinbeck, *L'istante largo* by Sara Fruner, *Il calamaro gigante* by Fabio Genovesi.

June

I spend my nights looking for books, new releases but also forgotten books—books that were neglected because of the implacable conveyor belt that carries titles on and off the shelves—two weeks of visibility and that's it. "Next, please." But there are readers out there who, like me, don't always chase the hottest releases. I've noticed, for instance, that for all the fanfare surrounding Carrère's *Yoga*, we sold only a handful of copies—while *Love in a Cold Climate* by Nancy Mitford, *L'istante largo* by Sara Fruner, and *The House in Paris* by Elizabeth Bowen continue to sell well. Here, people look for something they won't find elsewhere, something that won't disappoint them—here they *really* look. It's the aura that surrounds all independent bookshops.

Yesterday a group of switched-on girls picked up Reinecke and Schlieper's anthology of famous cats and their owners. I heard one of them explaining how the book was structured and I couldn't resist—I just had to butt in and tell them what I thought about the 27:5 ratio of male to female cat owners. The girls thanked me and put the book back. Two of them had just got married—as in, to each other. Luckily, Donatella wasn't around—she means well, but on these topics it's like she's been living under a rock. If they'd told her they were just married, she'd have answered, in all innocence: "And where did you leave your husbands?"

I have a friend in Lucignana who, like me, grows roses. His name is Romano, and as well as tending to plants and flowers, he paints. He never pretended to be anything other than he was, which is to say he came out to his parents decades ago—a pioneer, in short. His relationship with his mother reminds me of that of Pasolini with his own mother, Susanna. To me, Romano has always been a hero: those were hard times, and these were hard places, for someone like him. Anyway, everyone in the village knew, except of course Donatella. Romano enjoys books that track the slow progress of queer emancipation—a story that, before the happy ending of two girls in white gowns walking out of a town hall, was a tale of shadows and blood, shame and abuse. We could do worse than revisit those authors, because evidently, in a country like Italy where politicians can openly say that if they had a gay son they'd "chuck him in an oven," the battle is far from won. Here are a few titles I'd recommend:

- *Orlando* by Virginia Woolf
- *The Thief's Journal* by Jean Genet
- *Maurice* by E. M. Forster
- *Giovanni's Room* by James Baldwin
- *Nightwood* by Djuna Barnes
- *A Single Man* by Christopher Isherwood
- *A Boy's Own Story* by Edmund White
- *Middlesex* by Jeffrey Eugenides
- *Tales of the City* by Armistead Maupin
- *Call Me by Your Name* by André Aciman
- *Someday This Pain Will Be Useful to You* by Peter Cameron
- *Carol* by Patricia Highsmith
- *Fried Green Tomatoes at the Whistle Stop Cafe* by Fannie Flagg
- *Chocolat chaud* by Rachid O.
- *Flesh and Blood* by Michael Cunningham
- *Mentre la mia bella dorme* by Rossana Campo
- *A Girl Called Jules* by Milena Milani

- *L'altra parte di me* by Cristina Obber
- *The Well of Loneliness* by Radclyffe Hall
- *Fingersmith* by Sarah Waters
- *The End of Eddy* by Édouard Louis
- *Troppi paradisi* by Walter Siti
- *On Earth We're Briefly Gorgeous* by Ocean Vuong
- *Written on the Body* by Jeanette Winterson
- *Fever* by Jonathan Bazzi

Romano doesn't have all of these; I must tell him. And I must tell Donatella, too—someone needs to get her out from under that particular rock.

—

Today's orders: *Love at First Sight* by Wisława Szymborska, *Cortile nostalgia* by Giuseppina Torregrossa, *Malanottata* by Giuseppe Di Piazza, *Nomadland* by Jessica Bruder, *The Offing* by Benjamin Myers, *Long Bright River* by Liz Moore, *This Wild Darkness* by Harold Brodkey.

June 3, 2021

There was a silver lining to Mama being admitted to the hospital: for the first time, Pierpaolo and I are alone. At the beginning we had Laura, still so little, crying her eyes out if she saw me kiss him goodbye at Florence Airport. Then Mama started spending several months with us in Florence, from October to May, when she turned ninety.

Yesterday Pierpaolo surprised me with a trip to a wonderful place—Villa La Bianca in Vado di Camaiore. Today it's a boutique hotel with charming gardens, a swimming pool, and exquisite bed-rooms, but it was once the family home of the literary critic Cesare Garboli. He sold it in 1999, perhaps as his health began deteriorat-ing, and moved to Viareggio, right next to a highway intersection and the so-called Carnival Village, a series of warehouses where the huge sculptures for Viareggio's carnival parade are built. It seemed almost like a cruel joke concocted by his diabolical mind to tell us that it was all over: There will be no more Molières, no more Natalia Ginzburgs. We're just pretending.

I'd never been to Villa La Bianca while Cesare was alive—there was an aura of saintliness about that place; I was afraid of interrupt-ing some solemn ritual by treading too heavily on the grass. Many young critics would visit him there, including Emanuele Trevi, who wrote about his conversations with Garboli in his best work to date, *Sogni e favole* (Dreams and Fables). I, on the other hand, went to visit Cesare in his new house. I often wonder what is left of all that in this age of bickering academics and readers who are interested only in stories. The critics who most influenced my reading and my work operate today in a semi-clandestine manner, almost as hermits.

Villa La Bianca is beautiful, and the current owners, Massimo and Veronica, tread lightly, as if they were guests. They changed very little: the bedrooms are as they were, the kitchen was recently refurbished and now houses a huge photo of Cesare making coffee, so it almost feels like he is there with you. He was very handsome, Cesare—I forgot to mention that. I wrote a poem after I went to see him in Viareggio, where I picture him opening the door to me, like some sort of Marlon Brando in *Apocalypse Now*: finite, yet in-vincible. Massimo and Veronica offered us a few drinks under the old plane tree where Cesare used to chat to his friend, the writer and film director Mario Soldati. We'll be back with Donatella and

Graziano; perhaps we'll stay for the night—but not in the Yellow Room, which used to be Cesare's. Too many memories.

This is where I need Alessandra and her innate ability to bring everything down a notch or seven. She comes only twice a week now that Mama's in the hospital—I can manage most things by myself and she helps out with the laundry, the ironing, and the cooking. The last time she was here she made meatballs marinara and a zucchini quiche: A+, or "fucking delicious," if she says so herself.

—

Today's orders: *Il calamaro gigante* by Fabio Genovesi, *Historiae* by Antonella Anedda, *Tu, paesaggio dell'infanzia* by Alba Donati, *The Library at Night* by Alberto Manguel, *A Boy's Own Story* by Edmund White, *Almarina* by Valeria Parrella.

June 5, 2021

There are hard days at the bookshop too—days with few visitors, and none of them worth writing home about, the kind who'll hear about us and trek all the way up here just for a selfie. Yesterday two girls monopolized the Adirondacks for more than two hours, chatting and reading; then they left the books on the chairs and their cigarette ends in a plant saucer. One of them didn't even go in; the other had a quick look but evidently found nothing to her taste.

My mother was moved to a different hospital yesterday and I was told I wasn't going to be able to visit her. They also asked for permission to use a restraining strap to prevent her from jumping off her bed. Yes, I said. Yes, of course. The idea fills me with dread—a woman who only a few months ago walked the length and breadth of Florence from the gardens of Lungarno del Tempio to Piazza Pitti and back, or traipsed through the woods around Lucignana to gather firewood. Muted, relentless pain deep inside my heart. I'll have to tell her the story all over again of how she fell and broke a vertebra, to remind her I haven't abandoned her, to explain that there was no other way. But she won't understand and she'll suffer and I cannot bear her pain.

My mind goes to Annie Ernaux's *A Woman's Story*, to the different feelings she experienced when her mother died. Another fragile, modern daughter, another ancestral, rock-solid mother figure, another gulf between them. And guilt, too, flickering through it all, involuntary contractions of the soul that logic cannot defeat. Annie Ernaux is the author I feel is closest to my own experience of writing. Literature is nonfiction to me—a made-up story won't really grab me, or rather, it won't nourish me. Ernaux neatly folded away her life into various drawers: her childhood, her mother, the sister who died of diphtheria before she was born—a book for each major event or character in her life. I'd have enough material to fill twenty years' worth of writing myself. A rape drawer, a major illness drawer, a drawer for my daughter who as a newborn had to undergo open-heart surgery, one for my mother, one for my father—plenty of stuff to leaf through, in short.

Writing requires extreme care. It forces you to speak the darkness and at the same time see the beauty that blossoms within it. And you need to really pay attention. Beauty is less conspicuous: you need to search for it, wait for it, flush it out—but when it does come, it will floor you.

—

Today's orders: *Non oso dire la gioia* by Laura Imai Messina, *Il valore affettivo* by Nicoletta Verna, *The Summer That Melted Everything* by

Tiffany McDaniel, *Les Lendemains* by Mélissa Da Costa, *Chiara di Assisi: Elogio della disobbedienza* by Dacia Maraini.

June 7, 2021

My days start with birdsong: robins, blackcaps, goldfinches, skylarks, nightingales, chaffinches, sparrows, wrens, great tits, shrikes, swallows. Before the sun has even risen, they call out to one another, a lively exchange of precious information about food and shelter, routes and danger, which Pascoli so masterfully rendered in his poem "The Hammerless Gun":

> *And everywhere I go is a*
> *tac tac of blackcaps*
> *a tin tin of robins*
> *a zisteretetet of great tits*
> *a rererere of goldfinches*
> *. . . .*
> *telltelltelltelltell I hear*
> *(did you know?*
> *in the language of sparrows*
> *tellretelltelltell means*
> *come out! fly! it means*
> *run, boy*
> *it means danger!)*

Here Pascoli the polyglot effortlessly jumps from Italian to bird to English and back ("come out," "fly," and "boy" are in English even in the original, as is the poem's title). Pascoli was Italy's first true naturalist poet, the first to tackle inconvenient stories such as those of Italian

173

migrants in the United States—and to think that, when I was at school, his poetry was considered dated and quaint, altogether unpalatable.

At 6:00 a.m. I go out on my balcony to check on my sacred mountain, check that it's still there radiating its beauty, and, like Pascoli did with his Monte Pania:

I talk to him at dawn and many sweet things, I say to him.

—

One last glance at the jasmine in full bloom and I retreat into my tower, happy.

Sunday more than made up for Saturday's disappointing turnout—lots of visitors, all in love with the bookshop, all buying the books I'd have bought, which made me even happier.

I can't wait for Rebecca, my great-niece, to start her shifts at the bookshop. She's always been different from the other girls, quiet, a loner. The fact that she jumped at the chance to join our group of volunteers tells me there's something about her we don't know. The bookshop, meanwhile, keeps slowly but steadily eroding distances—our supporters are a more tight-knit group than ever. My parents are the old guard; when they're gone, it'll be up to us. Lucignana is a young village and we must live up to it—show the world we can rise again, work together, build bridges, and share a dream right here. Call me a visionary—maybe I am, maybe not.

—

Today's orders: *Central Park* by Guillaume Musso, *A Rose for Emily* by William Faulkner, *Cats, a Love Story* by Shifra Horn, *Mai più sola nel bosco* by Simona Vinci, *Nature* by Ralph Waldo Emerson, *The Year of Magical Thinking* by Joan Didion.

June 10, 2021

What a joy it was hearing Mike's voice calling out to me in his uneven Italian as he lugged two boxes of tea (which, clearly, made it through customs) up my street. His voice, the way he laughs, his Panama hat, shorts, and Birkenstocks, always put me in a cheerful mood. I was just about to jump into the shower, so I appeared at the top-floor window awkwardly wrapped in a towel—we were a Romeo and Juliet of sorts (and come to think of it, if those two had been sensible instead of getting into that awful mess they could have grown old together and enjoyed a lovely cup of tea). I recently found some exquisite teapots, too; as soon as they turn up, I'll bring out the treasures Mike smuggled in from Kent. Yesterday I also heard from Prudence, a lovely English lady who bought a house in Lucignana, and always shows up at the bookshop with trays of freshly baked cupcakes. She says she'll bring me thirty or so mismatched teacups from the UK. In case you hadn't noticed, it's always teatime around these parts.

Now that summer's here, with its calm and its delightful evening breeze, I'm more convinced than ever that if I had to leave this place I'd die. The landscape, yes—but the real magic is in the relationships. These streets are my home; with these people I can be the way I am, no need to add anything. Sometimes, like Mike, I walk barefoot—walk the earth, quite literally, feeling the earth beneath me, feeling the warmth of the sun, like a plant.

When I was little, there was a woman called Costantina, or La Gosti, as everyone knew her, who always walked barefoot come rain or shine, her unruly hair coiled up in a bun. She had always been old and lived in a house on the main square where no one dared enter. At times she would be screaming and raging at anyone she came across, at others lovingly caressing you with her large, gnarly hands, so we children were all terrified of her and would break into a run if we happened to go past her door. A child was left speechless for weeks after chancing upon her in one of her moods.

I never knew anything about her—whether she'd been committed when the Maggiano asylum was still open, whether she was ever young. She did, however, do this beautiful thing when the men carried the statue of the Virgin Mary in procession around the village: blond and ethereal in her light blue cloak, Costantina would draw hearts and chalices with flower petals on the streets. Meters and meters of petals—pink, red, white, yellow—which she carried in little buckets. She was one of the first street artists—before Natalia Rak, before Robson Melancia, before Mona Cameron, Lucignana had La Gosti. Maybe if she'd come across Tolstoy like the Russian farmer Anisya, today we'd know more of her ancestral strength turned savagery. Tolstoy, literary genius that he was, convinced his sister-in-law Tatyana Kuzminskaya to transcribe the story of a Russian farmer with a sweet-sounding name (Anisya), which he then read and edited without changing any of the facts. The result is a frightening snapshot of a time when women—and especially poor women—were believed to be worthless. Life as a never-ending string of sorrows, with no light and no hope of redemption. Yet Anisya and La Gosti feel like timeless heroes to me, two women who paid a high price for their independence.

When I walk barefoot on the rocks warmed by the sun, I feel their feral freedom, the freedom of Tiziana, of Alessandra, of my mother. I know that molecules of that same primeval strength endure in our blood—we are made of them, made of defeat and rose petals.

—

Today's orders: *Between the Woods and the Water* by Patrick Leigh Fermor, *Travels with Charley: In Search of America* by John Steinbeck, *Les Lendemains* by Mélissa Da Costa, *Avant de disparaître* by Xabi Molia, *L'acqua del lago non è mai dolce* by Giulia Caminito, *Sembrava bellezza* by Teresa Ciabatti, *Il silenzio è cosa viva* by Chandra Livia Candiani.

June 11, 2021

I was in Florence for two days, which is two days too long. Laura is finally done with her exams. The night before her final exam we chatted about D'Annunzio and Montale, about *Übermenschen* and lemons—old stuff that teachers always appreciate. They ended up quizzing her on Montale and she passed with flying colors. She was ecstatic, and I with her.

Mirto, for his part, is slowly but inexorably chewing through my beloved coat hanger, completely oblivious to D'Annunzio. I also took Laura to her vaccine appointment, which went well, then came back to Lucignana this evening with Pierpaolo—and now I'm too wired to sleep. Here every night brings the excitement of the eve of a big school trip. I can't wait for Laura to come to stay and join the other young volunteers—there will be four of them in total, with Rebecca, Sandy, and the newest recruit, Benedetta. Rebecca, incidentally, bought *Memories of My Nonexistence* by Rebecca Solnit, which makes me happy.

And our visitors make me happy too—they always surprise me, so enthusiastic, traveling all the way up here and leaving with armfuls of books that I chose with so much care. The review I'm most proud of is that of a nine-year-old boy who walked in and shouted: "Cool!"

Giulia and David, meanwhile, have left Palma de Mallorca for Costa Rica. We could use an enthusiastic couple like them to open a cute little bistro here. A few days ago, I spent an entire evening with Donatella fantasizing about what could be done with all the empty buildings in the village, especially the old school, the beating heart of Lucignana. Daydreams, mostly. But oh, what a venue: the things we could do with it! Medieval arches, colonnades, outdoor and indoor gardens, cloisters, a panoramic balcony, plus space for four or five large rooms and a restaurant. We've all been dreaming about restoring the long-abandoned school, which changed hands several times, although the owners never showed up. Should we just take over the building? Imagine the flower carpets in there if we still had our Gosti!

Tomorrow we're expecting fifteen girls for a bachelorette party and I've come up with a little game: I chose ten words from a poem by Beatrice Zerbini—we'll split them up into groups and ask them to write their own poems based on these words.

—

Today's orders: *The German House* by Annette Hess, *Canti di Castelvecchio* by Giovanni Pascoli, *Rosa candida* by Auður Ava Ólafsdóttir, *Quel che affidiamo al vento* by Laura Imai Messina, *Dept. of Speculation* by Jenny Offill, *Treasure Island* by Robert Louis Stevenson, *The Secret Garden* by Frances Hodgson Burnett.

June 12, 2021

We got to the last page of our MoMA *Lolita* notebook where I've been logging all the titles we've sold since we opened the bookshop on December 7, 2019. Next up is *Moby-Dick*; I'd love to start it on June 20, exactly five months after I started writing this diary. I'll log the titles we'll sell before then separately, then transcribe them.

I've also been working on a program for a series of events to be held at the bookshop throughout the summer—a miniature literary festival. I've called it Little Lucy (Lucy as in "Lucignana") in honor of all the Italian emigrants abroad and the Little Italies they built—places born of separation but also of the need for protection, for the preservation of shared memories. There will be three events in total, the first hosted by Melania Mazzucco, followed by Ilide Carmignani, and finally Abbot Bernardo will lead a "pilgrimage" from the bookshop to the Sant'Ansano hermitage, focusing on three keywords: "listening," "desire," "peace" (our priest Don Giuseppe will guide us through the woods).

Once upon a time, planning cultural events was my specialty—it just came naturally to me, like knowing what a "dash" of olive oil is. In 1999, I organized a large literary conference in Lucca and invited three emerging critics (Emanuele Trevi, Silvio Perrella, and Massimo Onofri), challenging each of them to name fifty authors who, in their opinion, had defined the century that was about to draw to a close. Their short lists would then be picked apart by more established critics, such as the great Cesare Garboli. On that occasion, Garboli shocked everyone by lambasting his favorite disciple—guilty, in his eyes, of "excessive romanticism" and "not paying enough attention to literary sources." The audience was flabbergasted: Chronos had devoured his beloved son. That night, I was later told, Cesare could not sleep.

While the tragedy played out on the stage, however, Trevi and the photographer Giovanni Giovannetti were nowhere to be found.

—

Today's orders: *Plant Revolution* by Stefano Mancuso, *What You Can See from Here* by Mariana Leky, *Les Lendemains* by Mélissa Da Costa, *The Hand* by Georges Simenon, *Chi se non noi* by Germana Urbani, *A Kiss Before Dying* by Ira Levin, *Un uomo pieno di gioia* by Cesare Garboli, *Summer in Baden-Baden* by Leonid Cypkin.

June 14, 2021

I've been to see Mike and brought him a bottle of white wine, which we drank on a bench looking out on the Apuan Alps. He spoke in English and I pretended to understand, but I did manage to convince him to read a poem from Edgar Lee Masters's *Spoon River Anthology* for our festival, on July 2.

"You need an American for that," he protested.

"You're the closest thing we've got," I replied. "You'll do just fine."

Laura, meanwhile, has graduated from school and is now a model (although I'm not sure who or what for)—I'm waiting for her and her menagerie to join us for the summer.

The bachelorette party was a great success. The girls were thrilled and all but cleared the shelves.

Flowers—I want more flowers. More *Primula auricula*, more *Primula pulverulenta*, more *Rosa gallica*, *Dianthus gratianopolitanus*, *Hydrangea macrophylla* hortensia, *Plumbago capensis*, *Paeonia officinalis*, *Lavandula angustifolia*. My climbing rose, alas, is suffering, and I with her. The leaves wither and fall. Not enough nitrogen? Too much fertilizer, water, sun? Is the pot too small? Misery comes in infinite shapes and forms, in plants as in humans, and it's so hard to find the right balance.

My mother's at the nursing home now. We can't visit her in her room, so they have to take her out on the balcony in a wheelchair, wearing a stiff neck brace—she's in a lot of pain and keeps whining. My brother, who went to see her with his daughter Debora, was shaken. Mama was in such a state that she never even opened her mouth or her eyes. How I wish I knew what a "dash of olive oil" is in these situations—the perfect balance that can make suffering bearable. I need Joan Didion's magical thinking, the kind that gets you out of a conundrum like not visiting your ailing mother versus visiting her and causing her more pain. My own magical thinking keeps telling me to bring her home, even with a broken vertebra, even if she could die. She wanted to die in my arms and I can't leave her on a balcony with her neck stuck in a brace and no house around her. I just can't.

In the evening I look out the window while the swallows dart in and out over my head, telling me about their nests, which they found intact. I listen, and cry.

—

Today's orders: *Emma* by Jane Austen, *Sense and Sensibility* by Jane Austen, *Elizabeth and Her German Garden* by Elizabeth von Arnim, *All Things Cease to Appear* by Elizabeth Brundage, *L'istante largo* by Sara Fruner, *The Murmur of Bees* by Sofía Segovia, *Sembrava bellezza* by Teresa Ciabatti, *Sinfonia domestica* by Tina Guiducci, *Empty Houses* by Brenda Navarro, *Nehmt mich bitte mit: Eine Weltreise per Anhalter* by Katharina von Arx.

June 15, 2021

Summer came, as it's been doing for a few years now, all at once and with no warning. The garden needs much more water, and often, and the iced-tea table (which also features Prosecco and spritz) has finally made its appearance, complete with a dainty little sofa fashioned from the base of an old wardrobe.

Dad will be back in Lucignana for a two-week "holiday" in August, when the village swells with prodigal sons and daughters returning to the fold. He can stay in Mama's room—it will be so exciting to have him home; it's not every day a father comes back after a forty-eight-year absence.

Mr. Wolf from *Pulp Fiction* comes to mind, the one who "solves problems." I solve problems too, except it takes me a lifetime and the problems themselves, buried under new realities, forget they were ever problems. Then, suddenly, the solution appears—the tear is mended, the pieces glued back together. Dad kissed Mama and Mama forgave Dad. I quietly worked away at it for years, and in the end, like Mr. Wolf, I cracked the case—a rather lackadaisical Mr. Wolf, I'll admit. The moral of the story is that if you just lie on a sofa and think the right things, the wrong things will take care of themselves.

This morning Giulia sent a message to the bookshop WhatsApp group:

Hello, does anyone know a Marino Donati? Was he from Lucignana, are there any living relatives?

Marino Donati was my brother's father, the one who went missing on January 23, 1943, in Russia, near Voronezh. The one whose name I bore for years, courtesy of our chronically misinformed Registry Office: when my father went to register the birth of his daughter, Alba Franceschini, he was told in so many words that my mother was married to a Mr. Marino Donati and any children of hers were to be registered under that name. I called Giulia and she forwarded me a voice message from a man named Leonardo who said he'd found a dog tag marked "Marino Donati" and "Lucignana" on a Russian website. The site is a marketplace for military memorabilia such as helmets, epaulettes from the Fascist Royal Italian Army, eagle-emblazoned badges, shirts that may well have been stolen from corpses—enough to creep anyone out. The tag itself, however, was rather moving—small and dented as if it had fought its own personal battle on my brother's father's chest. The auction started at one hundred dollars. I made an offer; now I have to wait five days and hope the tag makes it home safe, proof that a man had been there, that a father had died, that a husband had fought and lost against the Soviet winter. Ms. Wolf will bring home a fragment of that life, of those three lives torn apart by the folly of war, and will return it to a son, seventy-eight years after his father left for the front.

My own father, meanwhile, had finally managed to change my name—it had taken him thirty-five years, but we're not ones to do things in a hurry, as you will have gathered by now. The result is that nobody quite knows what my actual surname is, or who this mysterious Franceschini is, suddenly emerging from the musty archives of the aforementioned Registry Office.

Leonardo, from Carrara, is an amateur Second World War historian. When he saw the tag he googled "Donati + Lucignana" and he found the bookshop; he found me. He couldn't know I was the right person, the one who'd seen her mother cry on that name erased from history. Well, now the tag is on its way back, first-class postage.

On the website, the caption under the photo read "Бирка из бункера. WW2," which more or less translates as "dog tag from bunker. WW2." We could surmise that Marino died in a bunker (and what bunker?), but the tag might have simply been brought there after the war by Russian soldiers—we will never know. What we do know is that this tag belonged to a twenty-eight-year-old boy who saw his son only once before leaving for Russia, that it sat on his heart, and that it survived to bring back a token of his love.

1915
3 0294 (14) = C.
Marino Donati
Son of Silvio Donati and Santina Michelini,
Lucignana
(Lucca)

—

Today's orders: *The Way the Family Got Away* by Michael Kimball, *The Knockdown Queen* by Rufi Thorpe, *The Haunting of Hill House* by Shirley Jackson, *Once upon a Time in Hollywood* by Quentin Tarantino, *Cape Cod* by Henry David Thoreau, *The Nickel Boys* by Colson Whitehead, *Primeval and Other Times* by Olga Tokarczuk.

June 16, 2021

Today I've finally been to see Mama after the required two weeks from the first dose of the vaccine. I went up the external fire escape and emerged onto a balcony where Mama was waiting for me in a wheelchair—oh, the joy! She looked really nice—her hair had been cut recently; she was clean and well dressed; they'd even waxed the fuzz on her upper lip. But above all, she was there—really there, I mean. Sharp. "My baby girl, my baby girl."

She was very talkative, said she likes it there, people look after her, and she trusts Samantha because she's from Lucignana. My mother eats well and exercises in bed—puts on quite the show for the staff, I'm told. Leg up, then all the way back down to her chest, like a gymnast. I kissed her and kissed her in the June breeze, on the fourth-floor balcony of a nursing home.

Dad wants to see her too—another miracle. Dad is telling himself the story he wants to hear, which is that he loved Mama and would never have left her if she hadn't locked him out one night, to humiliate him. He didn't have a mistress, he was out with prospective clients, and she simply couldn't fathom that. She wanted a husband like all her friends' husbands—a farmer or a factory worker, or both. And that wasn't him. But like Marino's dog tag, their love overcame all obstacles, overcame time itself, and finally came home. I haven't told Mama about the tag, I didn't want to unsettle her, but I'll do it next time.

I listen to myself breathing in the clean air of Lucignana, the blossoming leadwort, the windswept horizons, and I feel my weakness turn into invincible power.

—

Today's orders: *Dept. of Speculation* by Jenny Offill, *Rosa candida* by Auður Ava Ólafsdóttir, *Canti di Castelvecchio* by Giovanni Pascoli, *La nostra Bloomsbury* by Vanessa Bell, *Too Much Happiness* by Alice Munro, *Sinfonia domestica* by Tina Guiducci, *Empty Houses* by Brenda Navarro, *Il vocabolario dei desideri* by Eshkol Nevo, *Il bambino nella neve* by Wlodek Goldkorn.

June 19, 2021

Rebecca has started her shifts at the bookshop, which is quite something, seeing as she barely ever leaves the house. She lives just outside Lucignana, in Sarrocchino, with her mother (my niece Debora) and her father, Fabrizio. Thin face, dark eyes, sharp tongue, Rebecca never really took to school, mostly coasted, doing the bare minimum. She doesn't get along with other girls her age, doesn't read, and the only thing she showed any interest in is the Italian rock band Måneskin. Her mother is convinced she won't last—she's "not a people person." But—there is always a but—we have Donatella.

I don't know how she does it, but she just radiates this incredible energy to which children and young people seem to gravitate—like that four-year-old girl who once spoke to her for about five minutes, then walked into the bookshop to tell her, "You know, I adore you."

Whatever it is, Rebecca is reborn. She read *Memoirs of a Woman Doctor* by the Egyptian author Nawal El Saadawi, and then posted this review on Instagram:

I often hear parents or teachers recommending books about love, friendship, life, to children. But why should children be interested in love, friendship or life from the point of view of a grown-up? If children or young people read books that are just wrong for their age, they will feel alone, they will feel *they* are wrong. I've experienced this myself for too long. *Memoirs of a Woman Doctor* grabbed me from the first page. I'd recommend asking yourself these questions after finishing a book:

1. Was it useful? What for?
2. Did I like it, and why?
3. Did it change the way I think? How?
4. Will it change the way I behave?

I'll start

1. I got a better perspective on a different culture
2. Reading it felt like myself
3. I understood I'm never alone
4. I mustn't stop fighting for my ideas

So there you have it—this quiet girl who barely left her room was just looking around, waiting for the right thing to focus her gaze on. Today she saw we'd preordered *Dos soldades* (Two Solitudes), a conversation on Latin American literature between Mario Vargas Llosa and Gabriel García Márquez, which will be published in

November—it's got her name on it. And then there's Angelica, who opens her window a few meters from our garden, shouting, "Mama! Come, quick, you can smell the bookshop!" When the wind blows from the west or from the south, in short from the sea, it carries our scent of amber and books right under Angelica's window.

—

Today's orders: *The Misfits* by Arthur Miller, *Moments of Being* by Virginia Woolf, *The Summer That Melted Everything* by Tiffany McDaniel, *The Wild Swans* by Hans Christian Andersen, *Casalinghitudine* by Clara Sereni, *Everything Inside* by Edwidge Danticat, *The Nickel Boys* by Colson Whitehead.

June 20, 2021

Giulia and David wrote from Costa Rica—they want me to go to Puerto Viejo de Talamanca to talk about one of my books. I get anxious about driving to Gromignana, let alone taking a twenty-hour flight to discuss an Italian poetry collection with a group of Costa Ricans.

And then again, Lucignana, Costa Rica, here, there, inside, outside—these are abstractions. It's all a matter of perspective.

That's what I should answer to those who ask what possessed me to open a bookshop in the middle of nowhere. The thing is, Lucignana doesn't know it's in the middle of nowhere; as far as I'm concerned, New York is in the middle of nowhere. This tiny village is to me the center of the universe, because I see it through the eyes of a little girl who braved rickety stairs and freezing houses in freezing winters, a little girl who tried to fix broken things as best she could. Fix, repair, redress—literature has an uncanny ability to make things right. "The redress of poetry," Seamus Heaney called it.

So yes, I opened a bookshop here, in this village that doesn't know it's in the middle of nowhere, because I had stairs, radiators, bathrooms that needed fixing—and I patched them up with books, the books I loved most. Now my own house is in order, I can start fixing other people's houses. And just so I don't lose heart in the midst of pandemics, various ailments, and fires, I'd better make a list of all the things that make me feel good. Lists save lives. They keep our memories alive, as Umberto Eco says in *The Infinity of Lists*.

Here goes:

- Laura's voice message letting me know she's at an LGBT+ rights rally like she'd tell me she was popping down to the shops, and warning me not to pick up if her boyfriend calls; he's looking for her, and fretting because he can't find her, and anyway, he "doesn't even know the difference between gay and straight"
- Raffaella's voice messages and her joy when she receives our books
- Maicol tearing through the cobbled streets of Lucignana, drunk on life
- My great-niece Rebecca joining the bookshop family, and the certainty her cynicism will blossom into something completely unexpected
- My father's existence
- The coffee I'm about to have with Tessa, who's on her way to us on her motorbike with a box full of bookmarks, our official bookmarks she's been gifting us since that day after the fire, with a quote from her mother, Lynn
- Emanuele Trevi and Giovanni Giovannetti absconding from the literary conference in Lucca, later found smoking weed

in a car in Piazza San Michele by a security guard, who happened to be the writer Vincenzo Pardini, so he let them go

- Ernesto and Mama cuddling on the sofa
- Daniele's Barbara and Maurizio's Barbara
- Ricchi e Poveri
- Donatella being sure Romano fancies her
- My mother trying to escape her hospital bed as soon as I look the other way
- Tina's mother
- Mike quickly wrapping a towel around his waist as I walk into his garden and Mike leaving Brighton with two large boxes of tea stashed in his trunk, concocting a story for the customs officers
- The anglers reading Louise Glück and Lawrence Ferlinghetti on the Segone
- The words I only ever hear in Lucignana: "lollers" and "slackies" and "bumming down" to pee
- My own continued, miraculous existence.

—

Today's orders: *Between the Woods and the Water* by Patrick Leigh Fermor, *Travels with Charley: In Search of America* by John Steinbeck, *On Overgrown Paths* by Knut Hamsun, *Il romanzo di Moscardino* by Enrico Pea, *Al giardino ancora non l'ho detto* by Pia Pera, *Walking* by Henry David Thoreau.

A Manifesto for Aspiring Booksellers

1. Live your life reading.
2. Welcome the people walking through your door as readers, not customers.
3. Never fancy yourself better than your readers.
4. Pay attention to what your readers ask for—it will open up new horizons.
5. Never betray your readers by recommending the wrong book.
6. Pick "your" authors and give them visibility.
7. Honor Sylvia Beach, every day of the week.
8. Always offer a cup of tea.
9. Flowers—don't forget flowers.
10. Remember to celebrate Virginia, Emily, Jane, and all the others.

Acknowledgments

Thank you to my schoolteachers—Fidalma Borrelli, Maria Laura Vichi, Rita Guerricchio—who made me fall in love with Elsa Morante and Cesare Pavese.

Thank you to Franco Cordelli, the best reading guide you'll ever find. Thank you to Vivian Lamarque, who was there, or always has been, perhaps hiding in the garden, unseen.

A (very special) thank you to the whole of Lucignana.

Thank you to Marco Vigevani, Claire Sabatié-Garat, and Chiara Piovan from the Italian Literary Agency, who believed in this book from the start. I will miss the Friday evening briefing and all the good news.

Thank you to Ernesto Franco for that Sunday morning. I can still feel that joy.

Thank you to the Einaudi crew: to Angela Rastelli, my guardian angel—I miss her "waves of dissonance" already. And thank you to Paola Gallo, Dalia Oggero, and Marco Peano for the energy they radiated (even via Zoom).

Thank you to Tina Guiducci, who reminded me, several times: "No, you can't say that—you're a poet!"

Another special thank you to Lucia Pratesi, she knows why.

A thank you I can no longer deliver in person to my parents, gone in the blink of an eye and yet somehow still here, defying all logic, making sure I eat, making sure I sleep, making sure everything is fine.

Thank you to Pierpaolo Orlando for his invisible presence, permeating every page.

Thank you to Laura, who lights up every word.

—

Finished on August 27, 2021, at 11:11 in Villa La Bianca, family home of Cesare Garboli.